SCAMS,
SCANDALS,
AND
SKULDUGGERY

SCAMS,
SCANDALS,
AND
SKULDUGGERY

A Selection of the World's Most Outrageous Frauds

ANDREAS SCHROEDER

M&S

Canadian Cataloguing in Publication Data
Schroeder, Andreas, 1946–
    Scams, scandals, and skulduggery

Includes bibliographical references.
ISBN 0-7710-7952-4

1. Fraud – Anecdotes. 2. Swindlers and swindling – Anecdotes.
3. Impostors and imposture – Anecdotes. I . Title.

HV6691.S34 1996   364.1'63   C95-933129-8

The publishers acknowledge the support of the Canada Council and the Ontario Arts Council for their publishing program.

Typesetting by M&S, Toronto
Printed and bound in Canada on acid-free paper.

McClelland & Stewart Inc.
The Canadian Publishers
481 University Avenue
Toronto, Ontario
M5G 2E9

1 2 3 4 5   00 99 98 97 96

Dedicated to the three CBC producers
with whom I worked on this series:

John Disney,
David Malahoff,
and especially John Stingecomb, with whom
I worked the longest, and whose remarkable ability
to recognize and shape a story in an instant
never failed to astound me.

Contents

Foreword

Somebody once asked Willie Sutton why he robbed banks. The holdup artist replied with admirable succinctness "because that's where the money is."

Not exclusively. As you are about to learn, there is untold potential wealth squirrelled away in all manner of curious nooks and crannies – from the Salad-Oil King's phoney tank farm in Bayonne, New Jersey, to Charlie Burlington's backyard pig sty (one sow, no waiting) in Okehampton, Devon.

"The money" is everywhere and anywhere. And all you need to get your hands on it is an absence of morals coupled with an abundance of *cojones*.

That, and a scam – some plan to fleece folks who own whatever it is you've got your eye on. Your swindle can be simple, outright robbery, as in the case of D. B. Cooper, who hijacked a

Boeing 727. It can be brain-numbingly complicated as in the Byzantine tax schemes of Oklahoma lawyer/fraudster Robert S. Trippet.

Andreas Schroeder has managed to sandwich seventeen of the most outrageous cons between the covers of the book you now hold in your hands. No mean feat – especially if you've met Andreas Schroeder. Given the company he's kept in this book, Andreas ought to look like a thug, but he doesn't. He is an elf of a man, with merry eyes and an utterly disarming smile. Andreas Schroeder is one of the mildest, most upright, uncrookedest men I've ever met.

I think.

No, I'm positive.

Why, I'd wager my deed to the Lion's Gate Bridge on it.

ARTHUR BLACK

Preface

———◆◆◆———

Few writers or publishers can afford the luxury of actually "bench-testing" a manuscript for readership appeal before publication. Scams, Scandals, and Skulduggery is a lucky exception.

Its origins date back to 1991, when CBC producer John Disney commissioned me to dig up a six-pack of particularly outrageous frauds for CBC Radio's enormously popular (six hundred thousand listeners) variety show "Basic Black," hosted by the irrepressible Arthur Black.

The stories proved so popular that he requested another six, and then another. Finally, we just decided to carry on until I ran out of material or the audience got tired of the series. Happily, neither condition has yet occurred.

It wasn't long before my mailbox began to fill with letters and faxes from listeners wanting to know more about the stories' sources, origins, and antecedents. Most of them asked if I was planning to publish them in book form. I wasn't, but as the requests grew, so did the idea. I began to track the number of responses I received to each story, and to widen my range from mostly literary to historical, financial, obsessive, and even religious fraud.

Scams, Scandals, and Skulduggery is thus a collection of seventeen of those stories that received the greatest listener response. A kind of "Best of Basic Black Scams, Volume One."

They're not, however, simply transcriptions of their radio versions. To fit the "Basic Black" radio format, each story had to be edited down to a ten-minute segment – the equivalent of about fifteen hundred words. All the stories in this collection have been re-researched and rewritten to approximately five times their original broadcast length. This has enabled me to get in right up to my elbows, and to do much greater justice to the complexities and ingenuities of each story. And for the reader who wants even more detail, there's a list of published sources at the end.

Three caveats. Since these stories range over a period of several centuries, I sometimes found the relative size of their thefts or frauds, expressed in original dollars, difficult to compare. To solve this problem, I have adjusted all the dollar amounts in these stories to 1990s values, using Statistics Canada's historical Price Index as a rough guide. This should give today's reader a more meaningful sense of the true financial impact of each scam, both in terms of the size of the crime, and the law-enforcement costs it engendered. (For those who prefer to just dip and taste, or who don't believe in reading Introductions, I've added a reminder of this caveat in each story at the first mention of a dollar amount.)

Secondly, readers should appreciate that stories of this kind are, by their very nature, inevitably reconstructions. They really happened, but sources often differ on many details. In choosing which to include and which to ignore, I freely admit to the motivations of a storyteller rather than a scholar. I have also taken the liberty of occasionally dramatizing scenes for which I had only the descriptive facts, and to quote, paraphrase, or even invent dialogue where I felt it did not misrepresent those facts. Since most of these stories were originally reported by persons who were not themselves participants in them, it seems safe to assume that any dialogue quoted in such texts was itself concocted by similar means.

Finally, an advance reader of this manuscript wondered, diplomatically, whether the collection's narrative tone – i.e., its fascination and even unabashed glee at the cleverness and outrageousness of these capers – might not fail to express an adequate indignation over the often-devastating financial effects of these crimes on their victims. That is a fair and legitimate question. As a responsible citizen, I'm sure I *should* be siding with the police, or at least with the judges, who had to deal with these miscreants. In fact, if I'd been one of their thousands of suckers, the smirk would have been wiped off my face *tout de suite*. I know that, and I admit it.

But, darn it all, they sure are an ingenious bunch of rascals, aren't they?

Andreas Schroeder
Mission, B.C.

Acknowledgements

A book of this kind depends to a very large extent on the kindness of librarians. My thanks to the staff of the Vancouver Public Library, the University of B.C. Library, the Mission branch of the Fraser Valley Regional Library, and the University College of the Fraser Valley Library.

Moreover, thanks to the many "Basic Black" listeners who kept me well supplied with the additional leads and suggestions.

Special thanks to my editor, Pat Kennedy, who saved me from many small embarrassments and probably some large ones, too.

And thanks, once again, to my family, Sharon, Sabrina, and Vanessa, for their patience and forbearance as deadlines loomed.

Running Away
with Mona

The Theft of the Mona Lisa

The Louvre in Paris is arguably the most famous art gallery in the world. That's because it contains, among its half a million works of art, possibly the most famous portrait in the world: Leonardo da Vinci's Mona Lisa, known in her country of origin as La Gioconda and in France as La Joconde.

In 1910 – specifically on June 12, 1910 – the Mona Lisa hung in the Louvre's Salon Carré, flanked on her left by Correggio's "Betrothal of Saint Catherine" and on her right by Titian's "Allegory." As usual, she was mobbed by a huge crowd of tourists, art lovers, and amateur painters, the tourists angling and shoving, while the amateurs desperately tried to keep their seats as they worked on their copies and imitations of The Lady. Making copies of the great masters was perfectly legal in turn-of-the-century Europe, provided the copies were either larger or smaller than the original, and clearly signed by the copier. During the first quarter of the twentieth century, there was a thriving market in Europe and North America for copies of the classics.

Two men watching this daily uproar from one of the salon's corners on this particular day didn't seem overly captivated by The Lady's enigmatic smile. They already knew that smile intimately. The tall, gaunt, soft-spoken man was Yves Chaudron, one of France's most accomplished art restorers. (Over the past few decades, Chaudron had also used his extraordinary talents to produce some of Europe's most brilliant forgeries.) His elegantly dressed companion, the Marqués Eduardo de Valfierno, had had the bad luck to be born the youngest son of one of Brazil's richest landowners, which, according to Brazilian inheritance traditions, had left him virtually penniless after his father's death. All Eduardo had inherited was a few roomfuls of art and the family name. But he had put both to profitable use, first selling off enough of the art collection to win the confidence of art collectors the world over, then selling them high-class forgeries when the genuine pieces ran out. Most had never noticed the difference.

"So what do you think, Yves?" Valfierno asked, flashing his trademark sardonic grin. "Could she be copied well enough to convince an art-obsessed American robber baron?"

Ordinarily that question would have been an insult to Chaudron's talents. But the Mona Lisa did pose a formidable challenge. For one thing, she was painted on wood, and fifteenth-century wood was hard to come by. For another, Leonardo had used a variety of vegetable-based pigments that weren't commercially available and would have to be painstakingly reproduced.

Finally, Renaissance painters had applied these pigments in so many layers, with so many coats of varnish and colour glazes, that a true replica involved a breathtaking amount of skill and work.

Chaudron, never much of a talker, threw another speculative glance at The Lady. "Probably," he shrugged. They had run this kind of scam plenty of times before. It was known as selling art "from the wall." An art collector with more money than morals was shown a famous painting in a museum or gallery and encouraged to make a bid on it "should it become available." For an additional fee, the museum's guards would be bribed to look the other way while the buyer surreptitiously marked the canvas on the back in a way that would later assure him he'd received the actual painting for which he'd bid. The delivery of the marked painting, plus some additional reassurance in the form of a newspaper clipping from the morning edition of *Le Matin* reporting its theft, usually guaranteed prompt payment and a delighted client.

What the delighted client didn't realize was that a fake copy of the original painting had previously been fastened to the back of that original, so that the "theft" involved nothing more than the removal of this client-marked copy. The newspaper clipping was simply a mock-up done by a compliant printer. Of course the scam worked best with clients who didn't live too close to Paris, where they might discover the abrupt "reappearance" of their painting in the same gallery or museum. In such cases, the client had little choice but to accept Valfierno's explanation that the gallery had substituted a well-executed copy to cover its embarrassing lapse of security.

The problem was, this was the Mona Lisa. To fake the theft of the most famous portrait in the world, you'd have to produce fake morning-after editions of almost every newspaper on earth.

"Which is why she'll have to be stolen in fact," Valfierno sighed. "And that will cost a great deal of money. We'll need more than just one good copy of La Joconde, Monsieur Chaudron. Make me four. In fact, make me five."

✦

Over the next fourteen months, Yves Chaudron bent to the task of making five exact duplicates of the Mona Lisa, while the Marqués de Valfierno tackled the delicate problem of selling them all as originals.

As ever, both produced first-class results. Chaudron's copies were so superb they even duplicated Leonardo's exact brush-strokes in many places. The Marqués, meanwhile, managed to pre-sell not five but *six* Mona Lisas "when she became avail-able." (What Chaudron had to say when he was handed that bit of news was not recorded for posterity.) Five were destined for North America, the sixth for Brazil. The selling price in each case, according to later rumour, was around $12 million.[*] With prices that high, suspicion automatically fell on the likes of J. P. Morgan and William Randolph Hearst, both known to be voraciously acquisitive art collectors. (Both denied the rumours indignantly.)

Once the copies were completed and safely shipped out of France, Valfierno moved on to the second phase of his scheme – stealing the painting. This, he was pleased to discover, wasn't

---

[*] For consistency, all dollar amounts in this volume have been adjusted to 1990 values.

going to be quite as complicated as he'd feared. The Louvre, in 1911, had surprisingly primitive security arrangements. This was at least partly because the original building had never been designed as a museum. It had been built in 1541 as King Francis I's domestic palace, and had been renovated and enlarged so often over the next four centuries that, by the turn of the twentieth century, its labyrinth of galleries and salons covered over forty-five acres. It was so riddled with hundreds of doors, staircases, courtyards, blind alleys, and service entrances that it had become a security nightmare.

Despite this, the Louvre's management had done surprisingly little to protect its treasures. From Tuesdays to Sundays, when over five thousand tourists streamed through the museum, there were often so few guards on duty that many galleries had no guards at all. On Mondays, when the Louvre was closed for maintenance, only a handful of guards remained to keep an eye on the army of white-coveralled workmen who swarmed through the buildings, hanging or removing paintings on instructions from the museum's many curators, framers, and restorers. Anyone dressed in a white coverall and looking like he was carrying out orders was unlikely to be challenged – no matter what painting or sculpture he was taking away.

It didn't take Valfierno long to find a former Louvre employee who was prepared to accept an offer. Vincenzo Perugia was an Italian carpenter who had once been employed – even Chaudron laughed when he heard this – making vandal-resistant frames for the Louvre's most famous paintings. He knew the layout and inner workings of the Louvre like the rooms of his own apartment. After six years as a guestworker in France, he also hated the French. They were, he'd concluded, tightwads, racists, and blatant snobs. Anyone with any sort of sensibility knew they were congenitally incapable of appreciating an Italian masterpiece.

And they didn't deserve La Gioconda anyway. Everyone knew that Napoleon had acquired the portrait by theft.

✦

On the afternoon of Sunday, August 20, 1911, Vincenzo Perugia and two compatriots ambled into the Louvre and began rubbernecking like everyone else. They were dressed as ordinary tourists, but each carried a bag containing identical white workman's coveralls under his arm. It was an hour before closing time, and the guards were beginning to yawn. The three men split up, but only to meet again fifteen minutes later in the Salle Duchâtel.

There, all three became absorbed in a positively reverential contemplation of a large Bramantino. While no doubt genuine – they were, after all, Italians – this fascination also had much to do with the fact that directly behind this painting was an artfully camouflaged door, leading into a small storage room. Perugia had discovered this room during his earlier employment at the museum. During the week it was normally used for the overnight storage of amateurs' easels, palettes, and other painting paraphernalia, but since it was Sunday, he knew the room would be empty.

Fifteen minutes later, during a moment when the salon emptied completely, Perugia released the door's concealed latch and the three quickly slipped inside. Using their bags, they made themselves as comfortable as they could on the wooden floor. It was going to be a long night.

At four o'clock, a system of bells began ringing throughout the museum, and its front doors were closed.

Twenty minutes later there was only silence, interrupted now and then by the footsteps of a guard slowly making his rounds.

The three spent an unpleasant night on the hard floor, trying to keep each other from snoring or making any other inappropriate noises. By six o'clock the next morning they had changed into their coveralls and were ready to join the workmen who crowded into the building half an hour later. They had to wait tensely until just past seven o'clock before Perugia judged it safe to come out. When they did, they were in luck – there was no one in the gallery.

For the next eight minutes, everything went exactly as planned. The three worked their way over to the Salle Carré, dusting and sweeping, until they were assembled directly in front of the Mona Lisa. Then, as casually as if it were an everyday part of their cleaning duties, Perugia's companions unhooked her from the wall, fell in behind Perugia like dutiful workmen following their boss, and brazenly carried her off through the Grande Galerie, across the Salle des Sept Mètres, and out through a service door.

The stairs behind this door led to the ground floor. At the bottom, an outside door led across a small courtyard to the Louvre's Visconti Gate.

Beyond the Visconti Gate lay freedom.

At the bottom of the stairwell, with his companions anxiously keeping watch, Perugia quickly sliced away the tapes that secured the painting to its frame. He kicked the frame, its glass, and then its vandal-proof box behind the stairs. He wrapped The Lady in his tourist shirt from the previous day, then waved everyone to the outside door. It was locked, of course, but the Marqués de Valfierno had given Perugia a copied key.

Then everything began to fall apart. The key wouldn't fit into the lock.

Perugia jammed and banged and jostled both the key and the lock. He worked the key back and forth, frantically, again and again. It wouldn't give.

Panicked, Perugia dug into his pockets and attacked the lock with a screwdriver. It still wouldn't give. He proceeded to take it apart screw by screw. The doorknob fell off into his hands; he stuffed it hastily into his pocket.

Suddenly, the door above them opened, and a man started down the stairs.

It was a plumber, carrying a tool kit.

The three froze in horror.

The plumber paused, saw the three, but couldn't make out what was going on in the gloom. They seemed to be having a problem. "You need a hand?" he asked.

Perugia, his wits back under control, instantly saw his opportunity. The plumber hadn't seen the Mona Lisa; Perugia had pushed her under his coverall as soon as he'd heard the door open. Now he vented his frustration in an outburst of Mediterranean temper.

"This stupid lock is broken; the doorknob's missing. How in the name of the Almighty is a man supposed to do his job when everything around here is falling apart?"

The plumber laughed. These excitable Italians. Every little problem was the end of the world. "Take it easy. Take it easy," he soothed. "Let's have a look at it."

He fished out his own key, turned the lock, used Perugia's screwdriver to lift the latch, and opened the door. "There you are. No cause for an uproar." He continued on his way, still shaking his head and chuckling.

Minutes later, Perugia, his cohorts, and the Mona Lisa were out on the street, pulling away in a cab.

✦

As Valfierno had hoped, news of the Mona Lisa's theft exploded across the globe like a tornado – though a tornado somewhat delayed by the fact that Louvre officials didn't even realize their most valuable treasure was missing until noon of the following day. Even then, suspicions were kept secret and an increasingly frantic internal search continued until the Mona Lisa's discarded frame was discovered in a service stairway between the first and second floor. So the Marqués didn't get his huge front-page newspaper banners until Wednesday, August 23.

But then, all hell broke loose.

Within hours, France's borders were virtually sealed off. Her ports were closed, all outgoing ships were searched, and all trains and railway stations were scoured. Premier Joseph Caillaux appointed a judge to head up an official investigation. When it was discovered that only eight guards had been on duty to secure the entire length and breadth of the Louvre that "Black Monday" (as the day came to be called), reprimands and disciplinary hearings mushroomed. Heads rolled. The senior curator of the Louvre and the Undersecretary for Fine Arts were forced to resign.

The evidence seemed to point to an inside job. Armed with a left thumbprint found on the discarded frame, police officers scoured their files, as well as the records of anyone who was or had ever been employed by the Louvre. This should have caught Vincenzo Perugia in a lethal crossfire, since he qualified on both counts: he had a file at the Louvre and an old police record for illegal possession of a knife. But, fortunately for him, the French police had adopted the inexplicable policy of recording only the *right* thumbprints of its criminals, and the Louvre had misplaced his file.

A second, more thorough, investigation, in which police officers actually tracked down and interviewed everyone who had been employed by the Louvre within the past five years, resulted in a police officer banging on Perugia's apartment door about three months after the theft. Perugia was interrogated for several hours, and the officer laconically noted that "according to information received it appears that on 21 August last [i.e., the day of the theft], Perugia, who is normally at work at 7 a.m., didn't arrive until 9 a.m. . . . . We have no explanation for these two hours of absence." Since it had been established that the Mona Lisa had been stolen during precisely that time-frame, such a coincidence might well have struck someone in the Préfecture de Police as worthy of note. It did not. Perugia was checked off the list, and the investigation moved on.

As per the Marqués's instructions, Perugia then retrieved the Mona Lisa from her cache at a friend's apartment, built her a more permanent hiding place in the false bottom of a toolbox, and stored this toolbox in the attic of his apartment, less than two city blocks from the Louvre. Knowing nothing of the Marqués's more complex schemes, he assumed that, when things had cooled down a little, the Marqués would open negotiations with Louvre officials for a sizable ransom. The Frenchmen would squawk, of course, being skinflints by nature, but when all was said and done – even deducting the hundred thousand dollars' advance the Marqués had already paid Perugia and his friends – he expected this caper to be good for at least another hundred thousand each.

Valfierno, on the other hand, had wrapped up his side of the operation with his usual finesse. Since he had shipped Chaudron's copies to New York and Rio de Janeiro well before the theft, he had been able to deliver them to his six delighted clients two weeks after the theft without difficulty. The $72 million he was rumoured to have received in payment was already safely salted away in several Swiss bank accounts, and the associated paperwork had been burned or securely hidden.

In consequence, he was now much less concerned about the real Mona Lisa than was Perugia; obviously, the longer she remained lost, the longer his clients would remain delighted. But that, for Valfierno, had become a merely cosmetic issue. By accepting his Mona Lisa under the present circumstances, each client had become, legally speaking, an accessory to her theft, and would be in no position to raise a fuss if the Louvre were eventually to claim her recapture.

And so, having no further financial interest in The Lady, the Marqués Eduardo de Valfierno and his partner Yves Chaudron quietly wrapped up their affairs, paid their hotel bills, and abandoned Europe to the gaffes and bunglings of the Sûreté Nationale de France.

✦

By November of 1913, Vincenzo Perugia was thoroughly brassed off. This was getting ridiculous. He hadn't heard from the Marqués in over a year. Could negotiations with the Louvre really be taking this long? By now all his advance money had been spent and he was broke. He wanted his remaining share of the loot, and he wasn't prepared to wait much longer.

The more he thought about it, the more irritated he became – at the Marqués, at the Louvre, at France. The Marqués was cheating him, he felt that in his bones. And the Louvre – clever dogs – had managed to turn their little problem into quite an advantage. More people now visited the Louvre to see where the Mona Lisa *wasn't* than had ever come to see where she *was*. Two years after her disappearance, people were still laying so many wreaths and flowers beneath her empty hook in the Salle Carré that the pile had to be removed twice a day. And France – well, the way France had treated him over the past decade, with its crummy jobs and rotten pay, he certainly didn't feel he owed anything to France.

An idea took hold. An idea that had always been there, just below the surface.

He would repatriate La Gioconda. He would return her to her proper home. Only Italians could truly appreciate La Gioconda; he had always said that to anyone who would listen. She belonged among her own, in Milan or in Florence. He had recently read an ad in a Florence newspaper, offering to buy art of any sort for "good prices." No doubt the Italians would be prepared to pay good money for La Gioconda's return.

When Alfredo Geri, the gallery owner who had placed the ad, received Perugia's letter a week later, its contents sounded so ridiculous, they gave him pause. Giovanni Poggi, director of Florence's famous Uffizi Gallery, to whom Geri showed the letter, had much the same reaction. But Poggi had experienced some pretty unlikely doings during a lifetime spent in the art world, and he counselled follow-up.

One month, two letters, and three telegrams later, the two found themselves in a smelly little room in the Hotel Tripoli-Italia on the Via Panzani in Florence, staring in amazement and disbelief as Perugia unwrapped La Gioconda and casually dropped her onto his unmade bed.

"My God," Geri breathed. "How much do you want for her?"

Perugia shrugged. "How about ten million lire?"

(This price, comparatively modest – about $2 million – but not exactly altruistic, was to prove a sticking point four months later when a Florence judge considered Perugia's impassioned plea that he had merely wanted to return La Gioconda to her rightful owners, the citizens of Italy, after her enforced centuries-long exile.)

Betrayed once again – after Geri called in the police – Perugia spent four months in jail, waiting for his trial date, while the rest of the world went into ecstasies over the return of the Mona Lisa. Once again, newspapers all over the globe were filled with stories about this famous portrait, and Perugia, with little to do but read newspapers, quickly sensed which way the wind was blowing. The average Frenchman was simply delighted to have France's national treasure back, but the average Italian was clearly extracting an extra measure of glee from the fact that a simple Italian carpenter had managed to make utter fools of the formidable French police.

The more Perugia thought about it, the more he realized he'd done just that. And, by God, at what risk! His story, to the press in the following week and to a somewhat less gullible judge four months later, was that he, Perugia, had masterminded this ambitious and daring deed entirely by himself, that his motives had always been nationalistic rather than financial, and that, if Italy was capable of any justice at all, he really ought to be rewarded rather than punished for so selfless a deed.

The press found this argument remarkably persuasive. So

did the general citizenry of Italy. Within days, Perugia was deluged with letters of congratulation, flowers, food, liquor, and money for his legal defence. By the following week, he had to be moved to a larger cell to accommodate all his gifts. By the time his court date arrived, even Florence's judiciary had got the message, and made itself enormously popular by announcing that Perugia would not be extradited to France. (The fact that France had never got around to requesting Perugia's extradition was not mentioned.)

The judge, unfortunately, proved less willing to surrender to this circus and sentenced Perugia to a year and fifteen days. This produced an uproar the like of which the staid judiciary of Florence had not experienced since the tax protests of 1885, and an appeal was hastily arranged. A more enlightened magistrate reduced Perugia's sentence to the amount of time he had already served while waiting for his trial, and the plucky carpenter was immediately released. He left the court surrounded by well-wishers and a press eager to make him into the hero he clearly intended to become.

The Mona Lisa, meanwhile, made her way back to the Louvre by way of a whistle-stop tour that paused in virtually every major city between Rome and Paris. Everywhere she was exhibited the crowds turned up by the tens of thousands. The crush often became a riot, and armies of extra policemen had to be brought in. Back in Paris, after much official pomp and ceremony, over a hundred thousand people squeezed into the Louvre in the first two days alone to catch a glimpse of the returned Lady. Finally, when the jubilation had settled a little, the Mona Lisa was moved into the Salle des États, where she still hangs today.

Ironically, it might be said that only The Lady ended up serving serious prison time for her part in this extraordinary caper. With the brief exception of Vincenzo Perugia, none of the other malefactors were ever brought to trial. Yves Chaudron, a master not only of forgery but also of avoiding the pitfalls that usually accompany success in crime, went on to live a quiet and financially secure life on the outskirts of Paris. Perugia's accomplices, though named in various police reports and publicly accused in the media, were apparently considered too unimportant to charge. The innocent (if greedy) Alfredo Geri, who tried to sue the French government on the basis of an old Gallic law that granted anyone recovering lost or stolen art a 10-per-cent "salvage fee," lost out on his windfall when the French government hastily passed a law proclaiming the Mona Lisa a national treasure whose value was officially judged to be "inestimable."

What Perugia had to say when he discovered that he'd been asking $2 million for a work of art conservatively valued at $3.42 billion was also not recorded for posterity, but at least he never had to pay for another drink the length and breadth of Italy during his lifetime. And none of the Marqués Eduardo de Valfierno's other accomplices (including, it was rumoured, an inside man at the Sûreté Nationale) was ever arrested.

The Marqués himself died peacefully in Morocco in 1931, well-heeled and still unshackled.

Only the Mona Lisa languishes behind bulletproof glass, chained to the wall of a temperature-controlled, humidity-regulated, and electronically burglar-proofed alcove. Every day she is besieged by an unbridled army of tourists and art lovers. When her spotlights are turned off at regular intervals to reduce ultraviolet-ray damage to her pigments, she is shrouded in a disappointing darkness.

Clearly, the Mona Lisa is doing life.

Robbing Arizona
to Pay James

———◆◆◆———

*James Addison Reavis and
the Peralta Land-Grant Swindle*

On March 25, 1883, the residents of Phoenix, Arizona, woke up to a nasty bit of news. Flybills and placards nailed to every telegraph pole in the city informed all landowners that, on January 1, 1883, the deeds to their properties had become null and void, superseded by a 1758 land grant that had just come to light and been duly registered with the Surveyor-General of the United States. Negotiations for quit-claims or rents for all deeded properties – on which their current owners were now considered trespassers – would be entertained in due course at the Ambassador Hotel by the legal holder of that land grant, a Mr. James Addison Reavis.

The burghers of Phoenix were not amused. An impromptu town-hall meeting rang with protests, denials, demands for explanations and legal protection, tar-and-featherings. The

Ambassador Hotel was stormed. Government agents were grilled and lawyers consulted. If James Addison Reavis had been foolish enough to show his face at the Ambassador or anywhere else in Phoenix that day, his negotiating might well have been conducted at the end of a rope.

All this anger – directed as much at the government as at Reavis – was particularly intense because a lot of people suspected, deep down in their anxious and fearful hearts, that Reavis's claim might well be legitimate.

✦

The whole mess had started in 1848, with the conclusion of the U.S.–Mexican War. During its aftermath, the U.S. government had purchased a 45,535-square-mile parcel of land ("The Gadsden Purchase") from Mexico for annexation to Arizona and New Mexico. However, an ancillary caveat also required the United States to recognize and protect all existing titles to lands granted to a variety of Spanish beneficiaries by the kings of Spain during the three centuries (1519–1821) that Spain had ruled Mexico.

And therein lay the problem. A U.S. land-claims office had been established that year in Tucson to adjudicate these claims – about three hundred of them – but its deliberations had been so slow that the U.S. government had lost patience and had begun selling off the new territory's land and mineral rights before all the claims had been discharged.

So far the resulting legal conflicts had – miraculously – been only minor. Some had involved claims for land that had been settled by Americans but then abandoned; it had been possible to quietly return these parcels to their Spanish claimants without much legal fuss. Where such solutions proved impossible, the government had so far been able to arrange land swaps or buy-outs to pull its neck out of a legal noose.

But Reavis's land claim was gigantic. Located mostly in southern Arizona, it covered over twelve million acres – an area roughly equivalent to the entire province of Nova Scotia, or half the state of Indiana. It included five counties, six towns, the whole city of Phoenix, the entire Salt River Valley, the Gila River Valley, part of the Southern Pacific Railroad's right-of-way, and a variety of mining enterprises like Arizona's enormously rich Silver King Mine. Over twenty-five thousand people had already established ranches, orchards, logging operations, and cotton plantations in the area.

A land swap of this size and this value at this late stage was unthinkable.

But so was the effect of the Sword of Damocles that now hung over the entire territory. Until this claim was settled, there wasn't a single land- or business-owner who could buy, sell, or plan his future with any assurance. At the same time, the value of everyone's investments was suddenly in doubt, and no one knew whether he might be evicted tomorrow, next month, or next year.

For some reason the territory's surveyor-general, a man named Royal Johnson, couldn't seem to appreciate the urgency of the situation. He added Reavis's claim to the already huge pile on his desk and insisted that it would receive his attention "in due course" and no sooner. He lectured the residents of Arizona on due process and fair play, and warned them that "every step in this very important investigation shall be a deliberate and well considered step."

This was not what the anxious landowners of Arizona wanted to hear.

Everyone who knew anyone in Washington used his influence. Letters and petitions flooded the offices of Arizona's congressional representatives. So many people wrote to and called on Royal Johnson that he had to barricade his door.

By July of 1883 the patience of the area's citizens – especially its bankers and businessmen – had worn out.

They sent a telegram directly to James Addison Reavis, insisting on an immediate, face-to-face meeting. They demanded to see what proofs he had for his devastating claim.

In a return cable from New York's Fifth Avenue Hotel, to which all communications for Reavis were being forwarded, James Reavis readily agreed. A meeting was scheduled for August 7, in the Ambassador Hotel.

It was the first bit of satisfaction Arizona's citizens had achieved in the five months since their world had been turned upside down. Now they were finally getting somewhere. On August 7, they were going to settle this business once and for all.

✦

When the contingent of politicians, bankers, lawyers, businessmen, and journalists were ushered into the Royal Arizona Suite of Phoenix's Ambassador Hotel at ten o'clock on the morning of August 7, the man they met was nothing at all like the brash, fast-talking carpetbagger they'd expected.

Tall, conservatively dressed, with a scholarly air and a gracious manner, James Addison Reavis was courteous, affable, and patient. He expressed the wish to be introduced to everyone personally. He shook everyone's hand individually. He answered all questions quietly and directly, and showed both restraint and good humour in the face of *Phoenix Gazette* editor Homer

McNeil's testy and occasionally intemperate remarks. He assured everyone that he understood their irritation and anxiety, and promised to do all he could to provide ways to allay those fears quickly and decisively.

He was not, he explained, of Spanish descent himself. It was his wife, Sophia Loreta Micaela, the last of the noble Spanish Peralta family, who was heir to the land grant in question. It had been issued by King Ferdinand of Spain, in 1758, to her great-grandfather Don Miguel Nemecio Silva de Peralta de la Cordoba, Knight of the Military Order of Carlos III, Knight of the Insignia of the Royal College of Our Lady of Guadalupe, and Gentleman of the King's Chamber. The grant, which also carried with it the hereditary title "Baron of Arizona," had been developed only briefly in the 1780s – problems with the region's Apaches had interfered – and the document itself had only come to light again several years ago. If the members of the delegation would like to examine it, and a variety of others the Surveyor-General of the United States had required . . .

Reavis indicated a large table under a nearby window which was covered with parchments, letters, and certificates. The lawyers in the group surged forward. For the next hour, while hotel attendants kept everyone supplied with refreshments, Reavis's visitors pored over these documents, the lawyers making extensive notes and carefully examining all the dates and signatures.

A few of the documents were photographic reproductions, but most were calligraphic copies made and certified by the Spanish and Mexican archivists in whose vaults the originals were located. Many of the latter were affixed with the seals of the governments of Spain and of Mexico. They traced the history of the Peralta family and its land grant through Spanish and Mexican government registries, palace correspondence, and parish records dating back more than a century. A packet of particularly old documents – copies of the earliest legal proceedings relating to the Peralta grant – were accompanied by a stained and curled letter from none lesser than General Santa Anna, former president of Mexico, certifying their authenticity.

When the seventeen men left Reavis's suite, after a generous luncheon and brief individual conversations with Reavis and the gracious Sophia, the lawyers looked worried and the businessmen looked sick. During the following month, they fanned out to claims offices and archives in Mexico, Arizona, New Mexico, and Washington, to investigate and verify the authenticity of Reavis's documents. Some researched the genealogy of the Peralta family. Some focused on the claim document itself. A lawyer for the Silver King Mine took on the job of looking into Reavis's background.

When they pooled their findings at a meeting in Phoenix in early 1884, the news was not good.

Nobody had managed to poke a hole in the Peralta claim.

The documents appeared to be genuine, and the paper trail for both the Peralta family and the Peralta land grant contained no obvious omissions or errors. Many original documents identical to Reavis's copies had been found in the archives indicated by him, and the records of issuance and certification for those copies also appeared to be in order.

The findings of the Silver King Mine lawyer were perhaps more intriguing. For a man now claiming a territory the size of a European country, James Reavis's background was decidedly modest. Born to a small-town farming family, he'd served without particular distinction in the Confederate army, then moved on to St. Louis to work as a clerk, a streetcar conductor, and a real-estate agent. It was while working as a real-estate agent and then as a developer in booming St. Louis that Reavis had made a tidy fortune, and it was during this phase of his life – as he was researching and registering land deeds and titles – that he had stumbled across papers relating to the gigantic Peralta land grant of 1758. They were in the possession of an American doctor, a George M. Willing, who had bought them from one Miguel Peralta several years earlier. Spanish claims were sellable and transferable, but the process proved much longer and more expensive than Willing had bargained for, and he soon found he didn't have enough money to go it alone. He accepted Reavis as a 50-per-cent partner, in exchange for the remaining financing.

As things turned out, Willing didn't have enough money *or* time. He died soon after, in 1874. Reavis promptly bought out his share from Willing's widow.

Reavis knew a good deal about filing Spanish land claims, but he also understood the odds against him. Any direct Peralta descendant could lay claim to the grant – or some portion of it – merely by proving his Peralta lineage. But, as a non-Peralta owner, Reavis would have to demonstrate the document's provenance from the moment it left the last Peralta member's hands, with proper sales and transfer records for each subsequent sale or change of ownership, right up to the date of his own purchase. That was a tall order.

Reavis had apparently decided to try both – to track the document's provenance, and to search for a Peralta descendant.

Four years later, in 1876, he reportedly found Sophia, the last living Peralta descendant, working as a scullery maid on a ranch in eastern Arizona. She was only fourteen years old and an orphan, and Reavis convinced her employer to permit him to adopt her. The rancher agreed, some money undoubtedly changed hands, and then Reavis entrusted Sophia to a California convent, where she remained until he returned to marry her in 1882. By then Reavis had also managed to establish the land grant's provenance, though this – as the lawyer for the Silver King Mine pointed out – in view of his marriage to Sophia, had now become technically unnecessary.

It was clear that Reavis had consolidated his claim to the Peralta land grant with a good deal of savvy and thoroughness. The claim had every appearance of being legally watertight. In fact, it was the opinion of the assembled lawyers that it was probably unassailable.

One after another, Arizona's bankers and businessmen began to book appointments with their new landlord.

✦

But not everyone accepted this verdict sitting down. *Phoenix Gazette* editor Homer McNeil pointed out in a rabble-rousing editorial that nothing was certain or official until the U.S. Land Claims Office had ruled on the claim – if Surveyor-General Johnson could ever be convinced to dust off his posterior and get to work. McNeil, for one, considered Reavis's claim to be unenforceable, and felt that the U.S. government would have no alternative but to rule against Reavis if enough people raised enough hell. He urged Arizona's citizens to stand up for themselves, to band together to fight for their rights; a man's right to defend home and hearth must ultimately take precedence over mere property laws; nothing less than freedom and democracy were at stake in this matter, etc., etc.

Such fighting words were exactly what his beleaguered readers needed. They provided hope and comfort when there seemed precious little of either. They also sold a lot of newspapers. Advertising, which had all but dried up with the news of the Reavis claim, sputtered back into life. The *Phoenix Gazette* became the rallying point for landowners who were not content or able to buy Reavis off with a quit-claim or a rental agreement. McNeil found himself cheered on and pushed forward; a leading position in local politics beckoned.

But his crusade came to an abrupt halt when the rival *Weekly Phoenix Herald* discovered that McNeil had actually been one of the first to quietly buy a quit-claim from Reavis – a contract by which Reavis had renounced his claim to McNeil's business and property for a payment of $10,000.

The news sent McNeil's paper into a tailspin. His sales plummeted, and his barely revived advertisement sales evaporated again. Even his widely reported withdrawal of the quit-claim did little to restore his reputation. Public support now swung over to the *Herald*, which became the official organ for Arizona's citizen revolt against Reavis. The *Gazette's* loss became the *Herald's* gain.

But McNeil's hypocrisy was probably more common than the *Herald* was prepared to acknowledge. Unlike the state's ordinary homeowners and small-business proprietors, who had little to lose by sitting tight and simply attending the mass-indignation meetings that flared up in many of the towns located within the Peralta claim, the banks and large businesses couldn't afford to put their operations on hold. So many of their activities involved the buying, selling, and developing of Arizona's land and resources that the mere possibility of having months – probably years – of business transactions reversed was a prospect too catastrophic to risk. Whatever their feelings about Reavis's claim, it made simple business sense to play it safe, buy him off, and hope to recoup the money later.

By 1884, the Southern Pacific Railroad had negotiated an interim rental agreement worth $8 million* with Reavis. The Silver King Mine had agreed to an interim lease and royalty payment of $4 million. Both corporations then sued the U.S. government for the return of the fees they had originally paid for their land and mineral rights. These agreements became the models for a flood of similar Reavis contracts with many of the area's other large businesses.

As the number of suits against the U.S. government increased, Reavis publicly offered the U.S. Attorney-General the option of buying him out – in effect, buying a quit-claim from him – for a lump sum payment of $8 billion. The offer was turned down. Like everyone else, the government was still waiting to hear from the Land Claims Office.

Meanwhile the anti-Reavis forces were having some unexpected luck. A plucky lawyer named Clark Churchill, incensed at a Reavis letter demanding rent for several properties Churchill owned in Phoenix, decided to grab the bull by the horns and counter-sue Reavis in district court. Since his Peralta claim was still being processed by the U.S. Surveyor-General in Washington, Reavis objected that the district court had no jurisdiction over the case. To everyone's surprise, the judge disagreed. He announced that, in view of the Land Claims Office's tardiness, and considering a number of weaknesses and omissions in Reavis's claim (which he listed), he would "settle the matter of the title immediately, rather than permit such claims to hang up forever to the prejudice and injury of the parties in

---

* For consistency, all dollar amounts in this volume have been adjusted to 1990 values.

peaceable possession of the land." He rejected Reavis's claim and granted Churchill a "quiet title" to his Phoenix land holdings.

Few people who knew anything about the law took the ruling very seriously, but it proved an enormous boost to the spirits of the citizens' groups throughout the Peralta claim. It also had the effect of at least temporarily stemming the flow of quit-claim agreements that Reavis had been managing to negotiate with an increasing number of its smaller landowners and businessmen.

But the ruling also had an effect that Churchill and the anti-Reavis activists had presumably not intended.

It gave Reavis advance warning, from a judicial perspective, of certain legal holes and insufficiencies still hampering his claim.

Not long afterwards, Reavis left Arizona on another fact-finding trip, to conduct further research in the archives and libraries in Mexico, Portugal, and Spain.

✦

When Reavis returned to the United States two years later, he had the air of a man who was not displeased with what he saw in his mirror every morning.

His trip to Europe, he informed a bevy of waiting New York reporters, had been successful beyond even his own high expectations.

He had brought back a whole trunkful of additional documents and letters, codicils, cedulas, records of court proceedings, and much more.

He now had copies of the Peralta family crest and its escutcheon. He had found additional letters and documents, mentioning or pertaining to the Peralta land grant. He had brought back copies of the birth and burial records of all the Peralta family members pertinent to Sophia's descendency claim. He had affidavits from her foster father and other acquaintances, confirming her Peralta lineage. But best of all, Reavis had unearthed a copy of the last will and testament of Sophia's grandfather, the second Baron of Arizona. In a special codicil attached to this will, the baron had specifically left the entire Peralta claim to his granddaughter.

The legal thrust of this document, Reavis announced, was so conclusive that he was filing an entirely new claim, this one based solely and entirely on his wife's ownership of the Peralta grant. And in view of the contents of the second baron's will, he, James Addison Reavis, was changing his name to James Addison Peralta Reavis, and was assuming his rightful title as the *third* Baron of Arizona.

While this news brought little joy to most Arizonans, it sparked considerable interest in New York and San Francisco. As high-stake gambles went, the Peralta claim had generated its share of boardroom discussions right from the start, but now it seemed to be gathering impressive momentum. The sheer scale of the gamble, and its breathtaking potential for profit, began to put a gleam in certain millionaires' eyes, and it wasn't long before the message box for the new baron's suite at the Fifth Avenue Hotel was stuffed to overflowing.

It wasn't mere landownership that interested Wall Street's financiers. It was the possibility of untrammelled state-wide development, without government involvement or interference. It was huge irrigation projects like the damming of the Salt and Gila rivers to create thousands of farms and orchards. It was the large-scale exploitation of Arizona's enormous mineral reserves, and the building of the roads and railways and telephone systems to facilitate these projects.

It was the fact that, in exchange for a share of the profits from all this development, Reavis was prepared to hand over all the undeeded portions of his vast territory for ten cents on the dollar.

It didn't take the baron and his backers long to come to an agreement. By the end of 1887, the Casa Grande Land Improvement Company of Arizona had become a reality, a company with an epic mandate to "construct and operate roads, railways, canals, dams, flumes, telephones, telegraphs, tunnels; to buy, sell, mortgage, lease, graze and improve lands, quarries and mines; to buy, sell and lease waters; to manufacture and mill; to raise and sell livestock, etc. etc." Its capital stock was epic, too: $8 billion, divided into half a million shares at $16,000 per share. The company's founders and shareholders included some of America's most prominent politicians and money-men: noted American lawyer and orator Robert G. Ingersoll; financiers Hector de Castro and Dwight Townsend; American Bank Note Company president Henry Porter; and Senator David Fergusson.

"No scheme of modern times has been supported by such an array of eminent public men and no undertaking has had such a vast amount of capital centralized for its success," enthused the San Francisco *Daily Examiner*.

As its first move, the CGLICA did what all rich men do – provided itself with a brigade of high-powered lawyers to smooth out life's little difficulties. It acquired (in addition to Ingersoll) Southern Pacific Railroad's crack legal beagle Harvey Brown, prominent New York barrister Ed Stokes, and

the brilliant orator and U.S. Senate powerbroker Roscoe
Conkling. Conkling especially was very thumbs-up about the
baron's prospects, and was even prepared to be interviewed
about them. "Having made a somewhat careful examination of
the ancient papers and other papers produced, of which there
are many, and on the facts and history of the case, I find they all
go to show Mrs. Reavis–Peralta to be the person she believes
herself to be, namely the lineal descendant of the original
grantee," he told an *Examiner* reporter. He was so convinced, he
added, that he had actually accepted the Peralta case on a contingency basis – something he had never done before.

As Reavis's reputation and influence grew, his inroads into
the world of America's business and political elite became more
extensive. He swapped directorships with California empire-
builders Collis Huntington and Charles Crocker. He became
friends with prominent St. Louis congressman James O.
Broadhead. He dined frequently with former president Ulysses
Grant and presidential candidate James Blaine.

They all liked his dignified-yet-affable manner. They liked
the way he listened – gravely and patiently. They liked his
thoughtful replies. And they were impressed by his shrewd
handling of his growing wealth. His origins were no secret, yet
he seemed so comfortable with money that he might well have
been born to it.

By 1888, Reavis's wealth was piling up like compound interest. He was still selling quit-claims in Arizona – the sales volume
had risen again after his triumphant return from Spain – but his
largest profits by far were coming from his growing sales of
Peralta claim investments in San Francisco and New York. The
backing of such widely admired men as Ingersoll and Conkling
was convincing dozens of other well-heeled entrepreneurs to

do the same. The New York manufacturer John W. Mackay climbed aboard to the tune of a million dollars a year. The industrialist S. A. Hurd signed up for a lump-sum investment of $5 million. Dozens of smaller investors contributed amounts in five figures, or bought large blocks of Casa Grande shares.

By 1889, Reavis was arguably the richest man in Arizona, and undoubtedly its biggest landlord. Thousands of residents were paying him rent, and dozens of businesses were paying him royalties. If a company was unable to raise the cash, Reavis was willing to take shares or a partnership, which made him a silent partner in many more Arizona enterprises. He presided over the largest private land-bank in the United States of America, and one of its largest land-development companies.

True: this rapidly expanding empire rested entirely on the legitimacy of a packet of yellowed parchments still lying unverified in a file in the U.S. Land Claims Office in Tucson, Arizona.

And true: virtually every dollar of this impressive empire was still being carried on everyone's books as "in trust."

But in most people's minds – even the minds of a growing number of Arizonans – such qualifications were fast dwindling into insignifiance. The reality was that dozens of high-priced lawyers had spent some of their best brain cells on the Peralta claim, and had rendered a unanimous verdict as to its authenticity. Some of the smartest money-men in America were backing it, and some of Washington's most prominent politicians had invested in it. If that didn't ensure the claim's legitimacy, what could?

By 1890, Reavis's business interests had expanded across the length and breadth of North America. He and Sophia now owned a mansion in Phoenix, another in St. Louis, a palatial residence in Washington, and a château in Spain. They were heavily invested in cotton, fruit, silver, copper, and vineyards.

Reavis's Casa Grande Company had commissioned sweeping surveys and engineering studies of most of the Peralta territory, and had begun to prospect for silver and gold. The Southern Pacific Railroad was building another stretch of track through the claim, connecting its Texas-to-California mainline with Phoenix. Slowly, step by difficult step, Arizona seemed to be learning to live with its Peralta troubles.

And then, in the spring of 1890, Reavis received an urgent telegram. It advised him to drop everything and come immediately to Washington.

Arizona surveyor-general Royal Johnson, it appeared, had finally – after seven years of fussing – submitted his Peralta claim recommendations to the Secretary of the Interior.

✦

To validate a Spanish land claim, the claimant had to make his initial application to the U.S. surveyor-general responsible for the region in which the claim was located. This official was required by an act of Congress to investigate the claim, and to make a report (with recommendations) to the Secretary of the Interior. The Secretary, in turn, was required to make any further investigations he deemed necessary, then pass the entire dossier on to Congress. It was Congress which made the final decisions on Spanish land claims.

Royal Johnson had never liked James Reavis. The two were polar opposites in both style and substance. Johnson was the ultimate bureaucrat: fussy, long-winded, and preoccupied with process. Reavis was a diplomat: gracious, good-humoured, and flexible. It's probably fair to say that each mistrusted the other profoundly.

Johnson's report proved to be a mirror of its author. Its

language was ornate and sardonic, its approach finicky and suspicious. He had many complaints about the Peralta claim.

His main objection concerned the fact that Reavis had not submitted (found) the actual land grant. True, he had found and submitted a wealth of tangential documents – letters and cedulas that mentioned the grant or took its existence for granted – but the point remained that the central document was missing.

Secondly, Johnson claimed – incorrectly – that no proof existed that the grant had ever been taken up. In fact, as mentioned earlier, Reavis had submitted letters showing that the first baron had attempted to establish a ranch at Casa Grande but had been defeated in his attempt by marauding Apaches.

Further, Johnson felt there was still insufficient evidence to prove conclusively that Reavis's wife and the Sophia Peralta described in Reavis's documents were one and the same.

Johnson also snagged on the fact that certain Peralta documents had been found in places where they didn't appear to belong, such as in books or folders containing unrelated materials. He also found it odd that the king had allegedly given this grant to Miguel Peralta in gratitude for "many services," but hadn't itemized them.

He found some discrepancies in chronology. He found some spelling mistakes. He said that some of the documents appeared to have been written with a steel nib rather than a quill, and steel nibs hadn't come into common use until some decades later. He pointed out that some official seals were missing.

For these, and a variety of lesser reasons, he did not feel he could recommend acceptance of the claim.

The report – leaked to the press in Arizona – caused an explosion of celebrations from one end of the state to the other. Flags were waved; impromptu parties and dances sprang up from

Tempe to Morenci, from Florence to Globe. The *Weekly Phoenix Herald*, which had hounded Johnson for years, apologized to him without reservation. The citizenry of Phoenix invited Johnson to a gala reception in his honour.

But cooler heads counselled restraint, and warned that this was just a skirmish in a much larger war. Two more stages had to be negotiated, and these were entirely controlled by Washington.

Indeed, Washington took its time considering Johnson's report. The Office of the U.S. Surveyor-General refused to comment. So did the Department of the Secretary of the Interior. Meanwhile, a spokesman for the Casa Grande Land Improvement Company pointed out in one newspaper report after another that Johnson's report was only a recommendation, and that his reservations were just that – mere reservations. There were no allegations of impropriety, no accusations. Quite possibly, a more balanced approach from a more disinterested tribunal was called for . . .

The Baron and Baroness of Arizona, who spent the next three months furiously busy in Washington, remained unavailable for comment.

When Congress finally responded to the Peralta claim, in March of 1891, the influence of Reavis and his friends – according to an outraged editorial in the *Weekly Herald* – was clearly discernable. Over the vigorous protests of the Arizona delegation, Congress had removed the investigation of Spanish Land Grants from Johnson's job description and handed it to a newly created Court of Private Land Claims, equipped with five travelling judges, a full complement of lawyers, and a scrum of investigators. This court was granted full powers to render definitive judgments on all outstanding Spanish land claims, and was under no obligation to consider local interests or concerns. Among the backlog of three hundred claims for which this court was made responsible was the Peralta claim.

A spokesman for the Casa Grande Land Improvement Company of Arizona expressed himself very satisfied with Congress's actions.

The Baron and Baroness of Arizona, looking quite cheerful when contacted at their Washington residence, now felt confident that justice would finally be served.

✦

The Court of Private Land Claims didn't get around to assigning an attorney to the Peralta land claim until the fall of 1893.

When it did, it chose a tough U.S. Naval Academy graduate named Matthew Reynolds, who had served three years in the U.S. Navy before returning to school to study law. He was now a highly successful attorney with a reputation as a formidable tactician.

Reynolds appointed as his legal investigator a Mexican-born lawyer by the name of Severo Mallet-Prevost. Mallet-Prevost was also a Spanish linguist, an historian, and an avid reader of Spanish literature. He was particularly familiar with the ornate and embellished language of the eighteenth-century Spanish court.

After a careful examination of the Peralta documents in Tucson, Mallet-Prevost boarded a train for Mexico City, on an 1894 journey scheduled to include San Bernardino, Guadalajara, Madrid, Seville, New York, San Francisco, and Santa Fe.

James Reavis, meanwhile, had made another productive tour of Mexico, filling in the blanks itemized in Johnson's report. He reported that he had finally found Sophia's birth records in San Bernardino, and had managed to track down an old friend of Sophia's father, who was prepared to testify that the Sophia Peralta he had known as a little girl was indeed the Sophia whom Reavis had married. He had found some painted portraits of Peralta family members and also some photographs.

But it wasn't until he had spent an apparently fruitless two weeks searching once more through the archives in Guadalajara that he had struck gold. In a bundle of records dated 1824, he uncovered probate proceedings relating to the first baron's will, a complete Peralta genealogy, and – most important of all – four cedulas, dated from 1744 to 1748, one mentioning, one affirming, and one actually approving the Peralta grant.

At this point his attorney, James Broadhead, who had accompanied Reavis to make sure that there were no more omissions, announced that, in his legal opinion, this clinched the case. There was no need to dig any further. He packed his bags and caught the next train for Washington.

Once again, Reavis arrived back in New York flushed with success, and once again Wall Street liked what it heard. More and more money poured into his myriad Arizona projects. He was now concentrating in particular on the plans to dam the Salt and Gila rivers, an ambitious project expected to cost some $2 billion. Reavis had already recruited two San Francisco entrepreneurs to commit themselves to $5 million of start-up financing, but he needed more partners. He spent much of 1893 and part of 1894 supervising the engineering and raising more investment capital in New York, San Francisco, and Toronto.

(In September of 1894, Mallet-Prevost boarded the train for a second trip to Mexico City, on a journey scheduled to eventually include Guadalajara, Madrid, Seville, and San Francisco.

This time he was accompanied by Matthew Reynolds and a judge of the Court of Private Land Claims, to take official testimony.)

Ironically, for a man who had spent the past decade searching for Peraltas, Reavis was suddenly up to his elbows in them. His wife had given birth to twin boys in March 1893, and now he received word that a group of 106 persons named Peralta – from California, Arizona, and New Mexico – had teamed up, hired a lawyer, and were trying to horn in on his claim. None of them were direct descendants of the first Baron of Arizona, but with $8 billion worth of property up for grabs, anyone with a sticky hand and the surname Peralta seemed determined to catch some flies.

Reavis ignored them. He had bigger fish to fry. He was hard at work amalgamating his various development companies into a single multi-branched syndicate that could synchronize his various plans more effectively and – most importantly – substantially increase the flow of settlers into his territory. The former, he was discovering, really couldn't proceed without the latter. He had already prepared a lavish brochure entitled "Barony of Arizona Open to Settlement" and was distributing it aggressively throughout the United States and even Eastern Europe, when word arrived that Matthew Reynolds and Severo Mallet-Prevost had tabled a bombshell report for the Court of Private Land Claims.

The Peralta claim, they announced, was a brilliant but completely fabricated fraud.

✦

Response to the Reynolds/Mallet-Prevost Report ranged from genuine shock and bewilderment to utter incredulity.

Of all the conclusions Wall Street had been prepared for, this one had not been on the list.

A claim lost to technicalities, to missing documents, to bureaucratic omissions or errors – even a slightly fudged entry here or there to bridge such gaps – *that* happened in land registries every day. And certainly, Reavis had demonstrated aggressive instincts for improving his position when the opportunity arose, and his marriage to Sophia Peralta had smacked of sharp business practice. But there wasn't a man on Wall Street who considered such manoeuvres anything but shrewd. The urbane, scholarly baron they had come to know and enjoy didn't seem capable of worse.

Dr. A. T. Sherwood, a San Francisco financier who had headed up Reavis's syndicate during the previous two years, simply couldn't believe it. "Reavis would have had to forge over two hundred Spanish documents and signatures!" he protested. "No man could have done it. It is the most improbable thing conceivable."

And yet, as Reynolds and Mallet-Prevost proved conclusively in the trial that followed, that's exactly what had happened.

All the letters, cedulas, court proceedings, and certificates of appointment relating to the Peralta grant had been forged.

The wills, testaments, codicils, and probate records had been forged.

The affidavits had been forged, falsified, or bought.

The birth, baptismal, and burial records had all been forged.

In fact, there never had existed a Don Miguel Nemecio Silva de Peralta de la Cordoba. He, and all his descendants, including Reavis's wife, Sophia, had been invented from whole cloth.

As had, of course, the Peralta land grant.

Whether Reavis had invented the Peralta Grant from scratch or had co-authored its earliest documents with Dr. Willing was never established. But certainly all post-1873 documents – some 196 of them – originated solely with Reavis. It was Reavis who invented the Peralta family's story, its genealogy, and its testaments. It was Reavis who found a young Mestizo orphan girl, invented a new life history for her, and cleverly braided it into his Peralta genealogy. And it was Reavis who wove everything into a complete tapestry, then spent a total of fifteen years travelling from archive to archive, church to church, library to library, and government office to government office, patiently replacing hundreds of original documents with forged ones, surreptitiously deleting and changing records where he was unable to insert substitutes, creating in this way the vast and complex paper trail required to make an entirely fictitious family officially real and certifiable.

Not that Reavis was a master forger. His ink lacked the iron found in most eighteenth-century inks, and his paper was rarely old enough for the century in which it was supposed to have been made. His efforts at eighteenth-century script weren't inspired.

But Reavis had reasons to believe that none of this would matter.

One of them had to do with the way documents were duplicated in pre-Xerox days. Though photography was becoming more common, the archives of Spain and Mexico still used calligraphic reproduction to duplicate their documents. A client specified which document he wanted duplicated, and a clerk trained in art and calligraphy laboriously reproduced the document line by line and flourish by flourish on high-quality archival paper. Such reproductions often looked more professional than their originals, with beautifully flowing script and impressive seals. Sometimes the clerks even corrected minor spelling and grammatical errors. The result was then officially certified with the archive's own stamp and seal, assuring officials elsewhere that this document was an accurate duplication of the original. Thus, an original document's blemishes and stylistic flaws – not to mention the age of its paper and ink – were no longer evident to a subsequent examiner.

But the next stage in the claim-submission process also played into a forger's hands. American courts employed interpreters to translate these documents, and these interpreters naturally strove for clarity, not literalism. A poorly spelled or awkwardly worded original text generally ended up sounding quite coherent in English translation – once again hiding its original blemishes.

So, in the ordinary course of events, the legitimacy of Reavis's claim would have been determined by non-Spanish people, examining beautified, corrected, and professional-looking historical replicas. A chronologically convincing paper trail of such documents should have won the day hands down.

This was the process Reavis had counted on.

What had tripped him up was the ornate language of the Spanish court. It differed markedly from ordinary Spanish, not just grammatically but stylistically. It contained idiomatic conventions that Reavis didn't really understand, but that Mallet-Prevost did. No translator would have expunged such conventions entirely, and Mallet-Prevost immediately noticed their absence. It aroused his suspicions and caused him to travel to Mexico and Spain to examine the originals.

After that, Reavis was sunk.

✦

On June 30, 1896, Reavis was convicted on charges of fraud, perjury, theft, and conspiracy. He was sentenced to two years in prison. He was also fined $5,000.

His wife, Sophia, was not charged. The judge decided that she was little more than just another of Reavis's thousands of victims. Soon after Reavis entered prison, she divorced him and disappeared with their two sons.

Reavis's other victims, however, lost little time in turning on him. A barrage of civil suits cleaned him out – in the words of Homer McNeil – "like a dose of salts." When he was released from prison in April 1898, he was penniless.

Reavis never recovered from his downfall. He would drift around the American west for another sixteen years, talking vaguely about resuscitating his Casa Grande Land Improvement Company to dam the Salt and Gila rivers – but it was just talk. Without the tailored clothes and expensive hotels, his patrician manner didn't have its former effect. In 1899, out of work and desperate for funds, he sold his "confessions" to a San Francisco newspaper for a paltry $750.

It was a sad and inglorious comedown for the architect of one of the most audacious and imaginative scams in the annals of forgery.

Reavis died in Denver in 1914.

Pot o' Magic Trademarks

Shamrock Shenanigans #1

The transformation of the Irish Free State of 1921 (a British dependency) into the Republic of Ireland (Eire) in 1937 was accompanied by plenty of confusion, disruption, and uncertainty. But it also brought about some unusual business opportunities.

It was Sligo barrister Sean O'Roarke who first noticed that, according to the new republic's constitution, British trademark law no longer applied to Eire.

Intentional or not, this little tear in Eire's new legal fabric had the effect of creating a trademark clean slate. Companies already selling their products in Eire wouldn't be affected, because a demonstrable history of use had always protected a trademark holder in Irish common law. Such protection, however, was no longer available to the makers of internationally known products not yet available in Eire.

Now, O'Roarke knew that many American corporations such as General Foods, Procter & Gamble, Coca-Cola, and Kellogg's were currently setting up subsidiaries, and were duly registering their trademarks, in France, Germany, Scandinavia, and England.

It stood to reason that, once they'd successfully established themselves in those more-populous countries – once they'd shorn the fattest sheep – they'd be expanding into adjacent, less-populated countries, too.

Sooner or later, O'Roarke calculated, Procter & Gamble would show up on Eire's doorstep.

So the crafty barrister got to work. Over the next several years, he quietly registered the trademarks and brand names of dozens of large American manufacturers – General Electric, Goodyear, Dupont, Kodak, Motorola, Honeywell, RCA , etc. – *under his own name.*

It was perfectly legal. Since none of these names had previously been registered in Eire, they were all, from a legal standpoint, originals. At the rate of three or four a month, it wasn't long before O'Roarke had acquired the trademarks of a veritable Who's Who of American business and enterprise.

It proved a profitable investment. When the agents of American consumerism finally showed up in Dublin to expand their empires, around 1946, they were stunned to find, one after another, that their brand names were already spoken for. In each case they were told to deal with a short, somewhat disheveled country advocate recently arrived from Sligo, who now owned the Irish rights to most of the world's most-famous commercial names. O'Roarke's slight stutter and mildly befuddled manner gave many of these agents the initial impression that he could easily be talked out of – or bribed out of – the powerful bargaining position he held.

But they were very wrong. Even before his new clients had begun to arrive, O'Roarke had made it his business to discover just how much it would cost a large international company to design new trademarks, recast its existing advertising campaigns, design new packaging, and produce it all from scratch in the Republic of Ireland.

It came to a pretty penny, and the negotiators – one after another – had to discover that, despite his scruffy appearance and absent-minded air, O'Roarke could bargain with the best of them. One after another they had to take a deep breath, grit their teeth, and pay his price.

From 1946 to 1957, his bill exceeded $50 million.[*]

To avoid being burned a second time, the Americans hastily fanned out across the remainder of Europe to register their trademarks in advance, even where no plans for market expansion existed. Apparently no one else had spotted the same opportunity as O'Roarke. Even so, the experience provided a major impetus for the creation of an international trademark convention – an initiative now on the United Nations agenda.

---

[*] For consistency, all dollar amounts in this volume have been adjusted to 1990 values.

Salad-Oil
King of the Universe

The Slippery Swindles of Tino De Angelis

All Tino De Angelis ever really wanted to be was the Salad-Oil King of the Universe. Failing that, he was willing to settle for Godfather of New Jersey. Being short, fat, angel-faced, and always hopelessly dishevelled made both propositions a bit of a stretch, but Tino's self-confidence and energy were limitless. He had ambition by the boxcar-load and smarts by the metric tonne, and it wasn't long before his natural gregariousness and deviousness saw him well launched in both enterprises.

The astonishing thing about Tino De Angelis was that he seemed able to make money no matter what the odds. Ordinary businessmen had to buy low and sell high; De Angelis could buy high and sell low and still make a bundle. He seemed to be able to defy the laws of gravity.

A few of the reasons for this were readily apparent to anyone even marginally familiar with De Angelis's background. From the minute he'd founded his Allied Crude Vegetable Oil Refining Corporation at an old tank farm in Bayonne, New Jersey, in 1955, De Angelis's file at the U.S. Department of Agriculture had swelled with complaints from Third World countries protesting his poor-quality oil, leaky barrels, and short weights. But De Angelis was shipping these oils under the American Food for Peace program, a gigantic giveaway scheme that combined foreign-aid initiatives with American farm subsidies, a pork barrel few American politicians were inclined to investigate too closely. For the few who persisted, De Angelis conducted his own informal "food for peace" program – ranging from exceedingly friendly persuasion to an army of lawyers with limitless funds for litigation. Peace was almost always quietly restored.

There were other allegations too: of Mob connections and money laundering, of Food for Peace shipments diverted into Western markets, of systematic high-level bribery. But even those shenanigans couldn't come close to explaining how an upstart young immigrants' son from the Bronx could take on a brace of giant Midwest oil-crushing companies like the A. E. Staley Manufacturing Company or the Central Soya Company – behemoths in their field, with enormous financial reserves and major shipping advantages – pay premium prices for their Midwestern oil, pay the extra freight charges to haul it all the way to New Jersey, sell it to America's largest export companies at prices the crushing companies could barely match – *and still make money.*

It was true that De Angelis earned and saved millions with his many ingenious business ideas. Rebuffed by the banks, he'd raised the millions he'd needed to establish his New Jersey operation by going straight to his potential customers, the export companies, and convincing them to lend him the money in return for unbeatable oil prices in the future. He'd saved further millions by storing and transporting vegetable oils in old petroleum containers – drums, tanks, even marine oil-tankers – pioneering the methods by which their insides could be cleaned and coated. His biggest application of this method was at his own tank farm in Bayonne, a leased subsection of a vast field of derelict and semi-derelict petroleum tanks, which De Angelis patched, cleaned, and converted for vegetable-oil storage. The tanks were cheap, in plentiful supply, and located directly beside a deep-sea dock and a railyard for easy import/export.

But of more impact than all his ingenuity and skulduggery was De Angelis's personal style. He was the original gladhander. He seemed to know absolutely everybody. He was effusive, expansive, frenetic, hilarious, colourful, sentimental, loyal, and generous. He could also be extraordinarily paranoid, duplicitous, vindictive, and thoughtless. But mostly he was irresistibly personable. He absolutely loved the business of doing business. Almost any business deal was better than no business deal. And De Angelis had the capacity to take the long view: a deal right now that gave his customer a windfall was likely to translate into a deal tomorrow in which De Angelis might be the major beneficiary.

He made a lot of deals like that, which made for a lot of happy customers. It also made for a whopping amount of business action, which made his bankers, brokers, lenders, and suppliers happy. Other happy people included a small army of cronies, retainers, and lieutenants, whom De Angelis positioned at all junctures of his corporate empire where discretion, secrecy, or a blind eye might be called for. These people were overpaid so handsomely that they all drove company-supplied Cadillacs, lived in company-financed homes, and enjoyed limitless expense accounts. To them, De Angelis was truly a godfather, a benign and remarkably thoughtful *padrone*, who always sent flowers on birthdays and anniversaries, asked affectionately about wife and kids (by name), and was known to have paid for an operation or a child's college education without even being asked.

Thus, the only people who might have been worried about life at the Allied Crude Vegetable Oil Refining Corporation – and its growing number of subsidiaries – were its accountants. But De Angelis made it a point never to employ easily rattled accountants. His chief accountant, a Mr. Alfredo Suarez, knew so little about bookkeeping and spoke so little English that his presence was only required to sign bundles of documents he never understood.

✦

The fact that the Allied Crude Vegetable Oil Refining Corporation was constantly borrowing money wasn't surprising to anyone. Almost all commodities companies did – even some large ones. It was in the nature of their business, which was cyclical, unpredictable, and generally feast-or-famine. Besides, Allied was a young company and still growing. Building up a company takes money.

Most companies prefer to borrow from the banks, but in 1955 De Angelis's credit history left a little to be desired. Before getting into the salad-oil business he'd tried his hand at meat-packing, and the results, from a banker's point of view, had not been confidence-inspiring. The Justice Department had charged De Angelis with selling uninspected meats and chiselling on weights; two New York banks had caught De Angelis kiting cheques and had closed his accounts; and, in the end, his meat-packing company had gone bankrupt.

So banks were out, at least for the time being. This had already forced De Angelis to come up with his scheme for borrowing money from a consortium of American export companies, and that arrangement continued to work well – but it had its down side. Not only did these companies charge premium interest rates while expecting "most-favoured" oil prices in return, they also maintained strict ceilings on the amounts they were willing to lend to Allied. It wasn't long before De Angelis was chafing badly at such restrictions.

It was at this point that De Angelis cooked up the "warehouse collateral" scheme that would make his name synonymous with mayhem and disaster in the annals of Wall Street for decades to come.

He didn't actually invent the concept. It had been around, in one form or another, for centuries. But the model in wide use in North America during the 1950s was enough to raise the eyebrows of anyone not totally naive about human nature.

It worked this way: any trader dealing in cyclical commodities often ended up with large amounts of product waiting in his warehouses for orders or shipments. This product represented tied-up equity and could lead to cash-flow problems. Traders in such commodities often needed bridging loans to boost cash flow. So lenders devised an arrangement whereby such product could be used as collateral against a short-term loan. The trader simply deposited his product in the lender's warehouse until he needed it back to fill a purchase order; at that point, the loan was repaid and the product released.

So far, so good. But this arrangement cost both the trader and the lender extra money. The trader had to pay the transport charges to the lender's warehouse, and the lender had to pay the costs of maintaining the warehouse. Much easier just to leave the goods in the trader's warehouse, but isolate or secure them in some way.

This too became convention. But who was to keep an eye on this collateral, to ensure that it didn't dwindle, or change, or completely evaporate?

Initially, the lender sent his own employees to do this. But these employees spent most of their time just sitting around; there wasn't much to do besides stare at a bunch of boxes in a room. And besides, they knew little or nothing about the goods being warehoused. So, in the next evolution, the lender simply hired some of the trader's more knowledgeable employees for the job, paying them either part-time or full-time to ensure the security of all pledged stock. (Business dictionaries of the day seem not to have included the term "conflict of interest.")

This final evolution became known as "field warehousing." Field-warehousing companies contracted with a wide variety of lenders to monitor and safeguard warehouse-based collateral on their behalf. They maintained records, guaranteed security, and – most important of all – issued the official warehouse receipts against which the trader could borrow money. These receipts assured any lender that the collateral supporting a loan truly existed and was secure in a warehouse under the control of the issuing field-warehousing company. (Nevertheless, the tradition of using the trader's own warehouses and his own employees continued.)

Obviously, the value of a warehouse receipt for securing a loan was only as good as the reputation of the warehousing company issuing it. So De Angelis chose the prestigious American Express Field Warehousing Corporation. American Express had a vast network of relationships with virtually all of the major banks in the Western world, and a name that exuded business prestige and financial stability. A warehouse receipt issued by such a company would be like cash in the bank.

Oddly enough – and it's unclear whether De Angelis knew this – the American Express Field Warehousing Corporation was losing money when De Angelis approached it in the summer of 1957. Actually, it had been losing money steadily since its inception in 1944, and an axe was already poised over its head. So De Angelis's approach came at a time when the company had to either make some serious money or go under. It didn't take AEFWC managers long to realize that the size of operations De Angelis had in mind was going to make the AEFWC some very serious money. In fact, Allied would promptly become its biggest account. The AEFWC – as hindsight would prove – didn't waste much time digging for information it might not like. It jumped into bed with De Angelis with indecorous haste.

This was the arrangement: AEFWC would hire three men from Allied's staff, all hand-picked by De Angelis, but all three paid full-time by AEFWC. These men would keep records and issue receipts for all oils deposited by Allied into tanks subleased and secured by AEFWC. (The tanks were simply labelled rather than physically secured by fences or barriers, since the amount of secured storage needed was expected to vary, sometimes more, sometimes less.) Every few months, an AEFWC inspector would drop by to double-check the records and physically check the tanks.

So this was how a man with a credit record so poor that no bank would touch him, and an inexplicably profitable practice of buying high and selling low, managed to rig up a financial vacuum cleaner whose hoses were soon sucking millions from the coffers of some of Wall Street's biggest companies. Lulled by American Express's stellar business reputation, a quickly growing array of commodities and credit companies now proved willing to lend De Angelis money to the limit of his warehouse receipts.

By the end of 1957 he had managed to borrow over $10 million[*] against such receipts.

By 1958 the loans had been boosted to $40 million.

By 1959 they had almost doubled to $75 million.

By 1962, after several brokerage firms had also climbed aboard this gravy train – De Angelis was still paying premium rates for his loans – his borrowings had risen to $225 million, backed by a whopping 480 million pounds of crude oil stored in AEFWC-secured tanks.

Once again, this produced a lot of happy people. The American Express Field Warehousing Corporation was finally making a profit, and its survival was secure. De Angelis's growing number of lenders were raking in premium rates for their loans. Some were even flipping them: lending money at exorbitant rates to Allied and then using Allied's receipts as collateral to borrow from their own bankers at far lower rates. The three custodians of AEFWC's oil tanks at Bayonne were enjoying lavish gifts from De Angelis for the good work they were doing, and various AEFWC inspectors and officials appreciated the profitable tips De Angelis passed on to them about stock-market

---

[*] For consistency, all dollar amounts in this volume have been adjusted to 1990 values.

deals he was about to make. No matter who you talked to, everyone agreed that De Angelis certainly had the knack for keeping anybody involved with him in a contented frame of mind.

True, there were problems now and then that might have rung alarm bells in the offices of the AEFWC. There was the complaint from the Scarburgh Company, whose independent inspector had found soybean oil in the tank that records showed should have contained Scarburgh's peanut oil. And there was the protest from the Bank of New York, whose inspector had discovered that a hundred thousand pounds of its cottonseed oil had disappeared completely.

Simple paperwork mix-ups, De Angelis assured them. It happens in the best of companies.

The errors were quickly rectified.

It might have worried AEFWC a little more if somebody had actually done some elementary math and discovered that the 560 million pounds of oil capacity now leased on paper by AEFWC from Allied already exceeded the actual capacity of De Angelis's entire tank farm by 60 million pounds. This wasn't immediately obvious, because Allied's tanks were surrounded on all sides by additional tanks belonging to other corporations – tanks either empty or being used to store fuels or chemicals. The AEFWC wasn't the first, and wouldn't be the last, to assume that De Angelis's operation was an awful lot bigger than it really was.

So De Angelis's loans continued to balloon unchecked.

By August 1963, AEFWC had issued receipts for an astounding 750 million pounds of oil – almost twice what the U.S. Census Bureau was reporting for the entire country. Luckily for De Angelis, AEFWC officials didn't read U.S. Census reports.

According to their regular audits and inspections, all was well and couldn't be better at Allied Crude. Records showed that since 1957 there had always been, and continued to be, more oil in AEFWC-secured tanks than was being used as collateral against Allied loans. Officials of AEFWC were so confident of this, they even loaned Allied $3 million against their own warehouse receipts.

By October 1963 – barely two months later – De Angelis's loans had grown to $440 million – secured by 937 million pounds of oil.

At this point, the sorts of rumours that had always floated around any De Angelis enterprise began to intensify. Though no one outside Allied had access to totals, it was becoming apparent from cocktail chat alone that the number of Allied lenders was growing like Topsy. Furthermore, the staggering amounts of oil pledged to some of the larger lenders was beginning to make them wonder whether Allied was trying to corner the entire market for edible oils – an illegal move that could endanger lenders almost as much as the borrower.

But the most alarming reports concerned the tank farm at Bayonne, growing rumours about fraudulent and forged warehouse receipts, cooked records, bribery, and shell games. Increasing instances of oil switches, mislabelling of tanks, and complete disappearances of oil were bringing more independent inspectors to Bayonne, and they sometimes found the tanks filled with little more than unidentifiable sludges. Curiously, corroborative inspections, sometimes as little as an hour later, invariably showed the huge tanks to be full of the correct oils in the correct amounts, which left the inspectors questioning their own sanity. The AEFWC stepped up its audits and unscheduled inspections, but found nothing significantly amiss.

What kept lenders undisturbed much longer than the rumours warranted was that De Angelis was repaying all his loans on time. True, he was paying old loans with new loans, and there was now such a blizzard of both that it took a growing army of clerks to keep track of them, but his lenders didn't know that. What they knew was that their loan collateral was being vouched for by one of the most illustrious financial corporations in the world, and that everybody was making buckets of money. Nor was De Angelis behaving like a man with money troubles. On the contrary; he was spending like a drunken sailor. He had two yachts moored at Long Island, a permanent penthouse suite at Manhattan's Sheraton-Park Hotel, a glitzy mistress whom he kept awash in diamonds and real estate and took with him as a "hostess" on his many trips abroad – De Angelis was living the life of a fabled rajah. And he wasn't keeping it all for himself, either. A steady dividend of largesse rained down on friends and strangers alike: a mail-boy at Allied had his mother's house refinanced; a retired government inspector found his medical bills had been paid. De Angelis genuinely enjoyed giving people a hand or helping them solve a problem, as long as it could be done quickly, and with money. "I'm a firm believer that he who does good all his life, that no harm will befall him," he once said – which, for De Angelis, was another way of saying he believed in buying insurance the old-fashioned way.

It's tantalizing to speculate how much longer De Angelis could have operated his financial vacuum cleaner without someone on Wall Street coming to his senses and turning the howling thing off, if De Angelis hadn't burst his own bubble in 1963 by losing his cool in the futures market. It proved a classic case of hubris, of pride coming before a fall.

De Angelis had negotiated a huge three-year oil deal with Spain in 1961 and had bought oil futures to hedge against any future price increases. When the deal unexpectedly collapsed, De Angelis found himself stuck with a lot of futures contracts he couldn't use. Instead of cutting his losses, he enraged the Spanish government and astonished everyone in the oil market by taking Spain to court. He lost the case, which took two years and an enormous amount of money to fight; meanwhile the oil market went into recession and De Angelis's futures contracts were becoming an increasing liability. But De Angelis couldn't let go. Instead of selling off his futures, he stunned the market by buying more – and more and more.

It made no sense. It was like bidding against yourself at an auction. Before long, De Angelis could only hope for a couple of truly gigantic oil contracts to absorb his futures, or a drought of biblical proportions. Of course there were people on Wall Street who were convinced De Angelis could arrange for either, or had inside information on the coming of both. But neither happened. And meanwhile, De Angelis just kept buying more oil futures.

Naturally, this took money. Truckloads of money. De Angelis's vacuum cleaner went into overdrive. The AEFWC warehouse receipts for Allied oil rained down on Wall Street in torrents. De Angelis put the bite on any and every company he could think of. He took money at excessive, then exorbitant, then ruinous rates. He began kiting cheques again, big cheques, cheques for $10 and $15 million. He bribed an accountant in the office of his biggest customer and lender, the giant Bunge Corporation, first to delay Allied deposits, then to mislay them.

By mid-November 1963, the Allied Crude Vegetable Oil Refining Corporation had managed to borrow a dizzying $1 billion, pledged against an utterly incomprehensible two billion pounds of edible oils – an amount so large, it was almost equivalent to the world's entire estimated commercial output for the international market that year.

On paper, at least, Tino De Angelis had finally become the Salad-Oil King of the Universe.

But only a few days later, on Friday, November 15, 1963, the price of oil futures dropped so sharply that Allied was faced with a raft of calls on its loans. The company, already hopelessly overextended, couldn't meet them. De Angelis tried desperately to power his overheated vacuum cleaner another notch higher, but Wall Street was finally waking up. The first domino in an empire built of dominoes began to fall.

✦

At first, news of Allied's insolvency didn't alarm its lenders unduly. Their loans, after all, were secured by oil safely stored in AEFWC-secured tanks and covered by AEFWC warehouse receipts.

But when rumours of alarming discoveries down at the Bayonne tank farm began to hit the street, many lenders sent down their inspectors just to make sure.

What they found at Bayonne totally ruined their day.

The tanks, they discovered, were empty – or as close to empty as darn is to damn. Those that weren't empty were full of seawater, or lard, or leftover sludge. Out of the two billion pounds of oil that should have been stored in AEFWC's tanks, less than seventy million were ever found. Of the rest, some had been illegally sold, some had been illegally switched – but most had never been there at all.

All the tanks, it turned out, were interconnected, linked by hundreds of underground pipes that crisscrossed the tank farm in a bewildering grid. Thus, a small amount of oil was all it had ever taken to keep up appearances during inspections and audits. As the inspectors had walked from tank to tank, in-line pumps had transferred the oil from tanks already inspected into tanks awaiting inspection. This could be done very quickly because it didn't involve much pumping; most tanks had been fitted with false bottoms or narrow cylinders attached to the inside rim of their inspection portholes. A dipper showing a full tank of oil was really only measuring the oil in a top-to-bottom tube containing a few hundred gallons at most. And it wasn't only oil that was missing. Whole tanks were missing, too – phantom tanks that existed only on paper, or that had been annexed without permission from the neighbouring companies that owned them.

The crash that followed, on Friday, November 22, 1963 (coincidentally the day of the Kennedy assassination), was so serious that the New York Stock Exchange, fearing widespread loss of public confidence in its brokerage houses (who were among Allied's largest lenders), closed the Exchange eighty-three minutes before normal closing time and spent the following long weekend desperately trying to sort out the mess. Fifty-two companies, a veritable Who's Who of Wall Street, had been sucked in by De Angelis's vacuum machine. Over a three-year period, he had bilked them of approximately $1.1 billion. Several brokerage firms had not only become insolvent, they had also lost millions of dollars held in trust for over twenty thousand small-time investors. In the end, the Exchange had to increase its membership levy to all Exchange members by 50 per cent to raise the $60 million required to rescue those investors.

De Angelis, meanwhile, dropped from sight for about a week, and when he reappeared, his companies' coffers – those of Allied and its many subsidiaries – were bare. Criminal prosecutors who tried to reconstruct his companies' records eventually decided that over $5 billion had flowed into those coffers over the previous five years, but no matter how hard they tried, they couldn't account for at least $875 million of it. Many of the companies to whom these monies had been paid turned out to have been mere paper entities run by De Angelis's friends and partners.

The Great Salad-Oil Swindle turned out to have been one of the most spectacular fleecing operations in American history, and it didn't stop with the bankruptcy of the De Angelis corporate empire. Having sold off the remaining Bayonne oil at fire-sale prices, government trustees were astounded to discover that several of the companies which had bought the oil were actually fronts for De Angelis's already-energetic efforts to resurrect himself in the salad-oil business. While pleading total poverty in the courts, De Angelis was already calling in the markers and favours that comprised his old-fashioned insurance policy – and his claims, it appeared, were being honoured without hesitation.

Nobody ever found the missing $875 million, though investigators did find at least one Swiss bank account containing about $2.5 million. There were undoubtedly many more, but in 1963 Swiss banking practices were still very crime-friendly. And while De Angelis was originally indicted on twenty-eight separate counts of fraud, forgery, and conspiracy, carrying a maximum sentence of 185 years in jail and a million-dollar fine, six months of clever legal wrangling and plea-bargaining reduced the charge to four counts of forgery and conspiracy and no fine at all.

On May 28, 1965, Tino De Angelis – still pleading total poverty but surrounded by an army of the best lawyers in town – was sentenced to twenty years in prison. He served only seven years. During his time inside, his cell was reportedly as busy as his Allied office had ever been.

✦

Update: Tino De Angelis was released from prison in 1972, but this did not end his scrapes with the law. Six years later, in 1978, he was indicted once again, this time for fraud in a hog swindle. He served three more years in prison. And, in August 1993, at the age of seventy-eight, De Angelis was sent to prison for yet another twenty-one months on five counts of defrauding Maple Leaf Meats of Canada of $881,000 . . .

The Flea That Roared

———◆———

The Grand Principality of Outer Baldonia

There are still a few old salts around who remember that glorious day of March 9, 1953, when their plucky little country, the Grand Principality of Outer Baldonia, decided to take no more goddamn guff.

It declared formal and unilateral war on the U.S.S.R.

"Yes, those were the days when men were still men, and fish were fish," Ron Wallace remembered fondly. "And there were plenty of both around." Wallace, erstwhile Minister Plenipotentiary of Outer Baldonian Tourism, had been promoted to Outer Baldonia's Ambassador Extraordinaire to Canada that year. "No kidding; the Outer Baldonian Navy stayed on red alert for four straight months," he recalled. "Right until the day the Tuna Tournament started."

It was an act entirely in keeping with the principality's manly and uncompromising past.

Located sixteen sea miles southwest of Wedgeport, Nova Scotia, the Grand Principality of Outer Baldonia is identified on marine charts as Outer Bald Tusket, a barren, unpopulated (save for a few wild sheep), four-acre mass of rock jutting out of the open Atlantic. Strategically located in some of the world's finest tuna-fishing waters, the island was bought in 1949 for $750 by one Russell Arundel, a mild-mannered, bespectacled Washington lawyer whose two favourite pastimes were tuna fishing and riding to hounds. The Grand Principality of Outer Baldonia was born a year later, in Arundel's fishboat on the high seas, on an afternoon when the tuna weren't running but the whisky was. Demonstrating the bold and fearless vision that would set Outer Baldonian politics apart from those of its more-tentative North American neighbours, Arundel and his friends roughed out a Declaration of Independence that included "the inalienable right to lie and be believed; to drink, swear, and gamble; to sleep all day and stay up all night"; furthermore, "freedom eternal from war, shaving, taxes, politics, inhibitions, nagging spouses and women" (insofar as they weren't the same thing), "suspicious questions, interruptions, sermons, and monologues."

Since there was some doubt that gender restrictions alone would ensure these utopian ideals, it was decided to limit Outer Baldonian citizenship to fishermen only – on further reflection, to *tuna* fishermen only; in fact, only to tuna fishermen who were princes or six-star admirals – though this was acknowledged to be something of a tautology, since all tuna fishermen are by definition princes and admirals. It was decided, nevertheless, to establish all this formally, and so, for its pantheon of Founding

Fathers, it was agreed that all sixty-nine members of the Wedgeport Tuna Guides' Association would be issued Outer Baldonian commissions as six-star admirals, their boats becoming units of an instant Outer Baldonian Navy.

No country is complete without its seal, and when Arundel arrived back in Washington he commissioned the Great Seal of Outer Baldonia: a tuna and a lobster flanking a wild sheep. This seal figured prominently on Outer Baldonia's official letterhead, and lent a certain grandeur to the washroom door in Arundel's office, behind which all official Outer Baldonian functions were performed. Its stateliness convinced a Foreign Services clerk to accept the new country's request for a listing in Washington's Diplomatic Telephone Book, and removed any difficulties in getting it added to the ground-floor directory of Arundel's own office building, Washington's World Centre Complex, where many foreign consulates and diplomatic missions were located.

It wasn't long before the phone started ringing. Arundel began to receive routine U.S. State Department calls "to all diplomatic missions," extending invitations to hundreds of public functions and requesting endless transmissions of statistical fodder. Then Outer Baldonia began to get mail – increasing amounts of mail – so much mail that a twenty-five-gallon garbage pail had to be acquired to handle it all. Within a short time, Arundel found it necessary to appoint Outer Baldonian ambassadors to both the United States and Canada, and an Ambassador Extraordinaire to the United Nations.

But it was the UNESCO request for a copy of Outer Baldonia's constitution that made Arundel realize he'd been shirking his regal responsibilities. He quickly arranged a constitutional conference with himself, proposed an official Constitution of the Principality of Outer Baldonia, voted unanimously for its acceptance, and registered it – festooned with all the seals, ribbons, signatures, and blobs of wax that any constitutional dictatorship could possibly require – with the U.S. Department of Foreign Affairs. This constitution vested all legislative powers in himself, King Russell Arundel of Outer Baldonia, but established as well a supporting hierarchy of Knights of the Order of the Blue Fin and a pride of Tunic Princes of the Realm. As a final measure, King Arundel ordered a supply of Outer Baldonian passports "valid forever and a day," and authorized the printing of Outer Baldonian currency, the basic unit of which was the "tunar."

Now a fullfledged country, the Grand Principality of Outer Baldonia issued a formal request to the U.S. Interior Department's Board on Geographic Names, and to the Canadian Cartographic Commission, to have its name added to all future North American charts and maps. It also forwarded its official latitudinal and longitudinal position to the Rand McNally Cartographic Division for inclusion in all future publications and reference works.

As any self-respecting country should, the Grand Principality of Outer Baldonia then began to exert its political influence by announcing its official position, via press releases to the United Nations press corps, concerning matters of international import: East-West relations, McCarthyism, the Korean invasion, and the like. Translations of these releases, and stories about Outer Baldonia in general, began finding their way into Europe and the U.S.S.R.

It is no longer possible to know, forty years after the fact, just what it was that so outraged the Russian state publication *Moscow Literary Gazette* about Outer Baldonia. Whatever the cause, the *Gazette* saw fit, in October 25, 1952, to publish a vicious and lengthy denunciation of Outer Baldonia's politics and policies, quoting excerpts from the Baldonian Constitution as textbook proof of the depravity and turpitude to which capitalism invariably leads. It accused King Arundel – this "Fuehrer of Baldonia" – of, among other things, urging his subjects to abandon all the ethical and moral laws that have sustained civilization throughout the ages. It claimed that King Arundel was turning his subjects into savages. It urged the rest of the world to turn its back on, and disassociate itself from, this vile little nation.

The article was distributed throughout the Soviet Union, but it wasn't long before a German translation appeared in Europe, resulting in an English translation that was published in several magazines in North America, and then as a reprint in several Canadian and American newspapers.

King Russell Arundel was shocked. In fact, he was offended and insulted.

No monarch worth his salt, no defender of traditional manly virtues, could let such a slur pass unnoticed. At the very least, it had to be challenged. King Arundel took pen in hand and, in appropriately ornate and considered language, delivered a formal protest to the Soviet Consulate in New York. He felt it incumbent upon himself to call the *Gazette* to task for this lamentable breach of diplomatic etiquette. Furthermore, he felt himself obliged, if satisfaction was not forthcoming, to formally sever all diplomatic relations between the Grand Principality of Outer Baldonia and the Union of Soviet Socialist Republics. And worse might follow. It was no secret that the Outer Baldonian Navy, based primarily in Wedgeport and a powerhouse in its own right, was also allied with the formidable naval forces of the Armdale Yacht Club of Halifax. A wink, under these circumstances, should have been as good as a nudge.

The missive was signed with his seal, "Arundel Rex."

Naturally, he sent copies to all the major newspapers in the English-speaking world.

The Russians rudely ignored the complaint.

The newspapers, however, didn't.

Inquiries began to arrive by mail, diplomatic pouch, and telephone. What were Outer Baldonia's primary exports? What had been the impact of the British atomic-bomb tests in the South Pacific on Outer Baldonia's sheep? What percentage of Outer Baldonia's GDP was spent on military installations? How many left-handed children had been born to Outer Baldonian mothers since 1934?

King Arundel had to hastily install a special Secretary for Outer Baldonian Affairs, a separate Outer Baldonian telephone line, and another desk. Running the Grand Principality of Outer Baldonia was suddenly becoming a full-time job.

The *New York Times*, the *London Daily News*, the *Atlantic Monthly*, the Toronto *Globe and Mail*, even the Halifax *Chronicle Herald* wanted interviews. Canada's *Maclean's* magazine made room for a special feature. The provincial government of Nova Scotia, pressed for its position, announced that it was considering formal recognition of this spunky little country.

But the Russians refused to pick up the gauntlet.

Finally, after a more-than-reasonable interval, and after due and lengthy consultations with his Knights of the Order of the Blue Fin and his Tunic Princes of the Realm, King Arundel was left with no other honourable option. He closed Outer Baldonia's borders to all international traffic, ordered the Outer Baldonian Navy to full alert, and, on March 9, 1953, issued to the Soviet Union a formal declaration of war.

Anxious and politically dangerous days followed. It was the

height of the Cold War, and East-West relations were at an all-time low. There were fears that this altercation might draw in other nations. Another worldwide outbreak of hostilities was not out of the question. Letters and telephone calls flashed back and forth between Moscow and its diplomatic missions. Everyone waited breathlessly for the next Russian move.

When it came, it came with Machiavellian simplicity. Long-time experts in the military tactic of total denial, the Russians decided to act as if nothing had happened. They did not reply to Outer Baldonia's declaration. They feigned ignorance when questioned by the press. They blocked the story entirely from Russia's airwaves and newspapers. They even managed to keep the issue off the agenda of the United Nations Security Council.

Undeceived, the Outer Baldonian Navy remained on full alert for four entire months. Its sixty-nine trawlers, schooners, doggers, yawls, drifters, dories, and rowboats stood ready to slip their moorings at a moment's notice. Its admirals patrolled the pubs and marinas of Yarmouth, Wedgeport, Lunenburg, and Halifax with relentless diligence.

The strategy proved an incontestable success. No Soviet naval vessel dared approach within two hundred miles of Outer Baldonia's shores. No point on Outer Baldonia's coastline was ever torpedoed or bombed. All KGB efforts to infiltrate Outer Baldonia's government bureaucracy failed. As later events would prove, the Soviets did begin delivering secret shiploads of arms and rocketry to Cuba under cover of night, but, by the time they were eventually ready to deploy them against Outer Baldonia, the operation was sidetracked by the U.S. invasion of the Bay of Pigs.

Years after the initial crisis, Baldonian Ambassador Extraordinaire Ron Wallace admitted that the frenzied adulation of the Outer

Baldonian citizenry at this unprecedented victory may have gone to Arundel's head, and even contributed to "Old Baldy's" (as it became known) eventual demise. "The country peaked too soon," he sighed. "It was hard for Arundel to come up with an encore."

During the following decade, internal strife often distracted Outer Baldonia from its political responsibilities as commentator on world events. A constitutional crisis developed when Arundel, without consulting his knights and princes, caused a large sign to be erected on Outer Baldonia's eastern shoreline reading: FISHERMEN ARE NOT TO PET THE SHEEP! "We were all shocked at the brazen authoritarianism of it," Wallace recalled, shaking his head. "It was in blatant violation of Clause 4A of the Constitution — freedom from nagging, interruptions, politics — not to mention inhibitions!"

Other scandals followed. At one point Arundel stood accused of having shamelessly squandered Outer Baldonia's hard-won international prestige by misusing his regal influence to convince ("force," his accusers insisted) the flight crew of Air Canada's flight 622 from Halifax to New York to permit him to carry a 150-pound tuna on board as cabin baggage. The incident, alleged to have taken place on the last day of Outer Baldonia's Sixth Annual Tuna Tournament, reportedly resulted in several crisp exchanges between the Canadian High Commission and Outer Baldonia's Foreign Affairs Department.

But the most disastrous blow to Outer Baldonia's international reputation for masculine integrity occurred when one of the country's own six-star admirals, Jean-Luc McGillicutty of Liverpool, Nova Scotia, reported upon his return from a three-day tuna-fishing expedition off the grand banks of Outer Baldonia that he had sighted King Arundel's fishing sloop at anchor less than a mile off Outer Baldonia's south-facing cliffs, and, on the foredeck, clearly visible to anyone with a set of 7 x 50 binoculars, had been a person of the female persuasion – in gross and flagrant contravention of Outer Baldonia's constitutional guarantee to all its citizens of "freedom eternal from nagging spouses and women" (Clause 5C).

This holed Outer Baldonia's ship of state below the waterline. It began to take on serious water. Though King Arundel protested that his spouse hadn't been nagging, indeed had never nagged – a claim so absurd he promptly had to invoke his right, according to constitutional guarantee 7A, "to lie and be believed" – the damage was irreparable. Civil unrest ensued. Half the Outer Baldonian Navy mutinied and flew their flags at half-mast; the other half opened their hatches and gangplanks to a wave of female boarders, who, to the horror of Outer Baldonia's older veterans, sometimes caught more fish than the men.

Whether or not even this disaster might have been survived became a moot point when the tuna began to dwindle in the 1960s. Fewer and fewer princes and admirals called in at Old Baldy to pet the sheep. The country's coffers emptied and were not refilled. Ron Wallace finally saw no other alternative but to resign his commission as Outer Baldonia's exalted Ambassador Extraordinaire to Canada and accept the lowly job of Lord Mayor of Halifax, Nova Scotia.

Finally, in 1975, a swan-song press release from King Russell Arundel himself sealed the Grand Principality of Outer Baldonia's fate. Having concluded that his country was now for the birds, King Arundel generously deeded Outer Baldonia to the Nova Scotia Bird Society for the royal sum of one tunar.

The NSBS promptly proclaimed Old Baldy an official bird sanctuary.

Pig in a Poke

———◆◆———

A British Hornswoggle

It was reportedly during the prosperous fifties that Britain's working class became Britain's middle class: people who for the first time in their lives actually had a little money left over after paying the rent, the grocer, and the bank. But what to do with that money? This became, for many, a considerably more complex problem than they'd ever thought possible.

Saving it for a rainy day – God knows there'd been enough of them during the previous decade – came most easily to mind. But while it was being saved, they wanted that money to be earning good interest. Such instincts are common to everyone. But the banks in the fifties weren't paying high interest – one of the causes of all this prosperity. So the middle class cast about for more profitable investments.

The stock market, of course, was out of the question. That was for toffs and rounders. Nobody in his right mind risked his hard-earned savings in shark-pools of that kind. On the other hand, the glittering chimera of something for nothing, of the big lottery-like score – the sort of thing a fistful of extra money made possible – proved awfully tempting. The problem was where to find such an opportunity in a venture that was straightforward, hugely profitable – and safe.

The solution appeared in the *Times* of October 28, 1958. In a modest advertisement, the Westminster-on-Tyne Livestock Company announced an investment opportunity for the "lay investor" that was both unique and very profitable. All it required was an outlay of £100 (about $250) per porcine unit.*

Shorn of its rhetoric, the investment opportunity boiled down to this: you invested in your own personal pig, or, more precisely, your own personal sow. The Westminster-on-Tyne Livestock Company would buy the sow, raise her, and breed her. The profits from the resulting piglets – also raised and sold by the WOTLC on the investor's behalf – would be shared fifty-fifty between the investor and the WOTLC. It was expected that most sows would produce two litters per year.

It was simple, profitable, and safe – and there were further reassuring features. Every investor was promised a full set of legally notarized ownership papers for each sow. If he preferred, an investor could even provide a name for his pig. A colour photo of each pig would be appended to the ownership papers. Biannual reports would keep him up to date on his investment's

---

* For consistency, all dollar amounts in this volume have been adjusted to 1990 values.

health, progress, and vital statistics. The prospects for high profits were excellent, since the Westminster-on-Tyne Livestock Company was "the most modern pig-farm in Europe," using all the latest pig-breeding methods and technologies. And the market for pork was strong.

This was just what the doctor had ordered. Response to the ad was immediate and overwhelming. Over the next eighteen months, almost three thousand wage-earners from all over England became armchair farmers, investing over £1.2 million – almost $3 million – in WOTLC's pig-raising venture. All promptly received their ownership papers, photographs, and progress reports. All basked in the news that their pigs were growing splendidly, their litters had been large, and the market for pork was still rising. All, presumably, now viewed their morning bangers and mash with a subtly changed, slightly more entrepreneurial, eye.

It was at the eighteen-month stage, around the fall of 1960, that the flow of investment dollars began to falter. At the same time, demand for answers grew. Even armchair farmers realized that the gestation period for a sow, multiplied by two litters per year, ought to have resulted in at least *some* initial returns. Queries to the Westminster-on-Tyne Livestock Company brought boiler-plate letters acknowledging that "some returns on investments have not been received on the dates expected," and that "our administrative procedures require overhauling and speeding up." As more months passed, it became obvious that the WOTLC needed fewer administrative procedures and a lot more financial reporting. Not to mention the coughing up of some serious boodle.

No coughing-up occurred, and in January of 1961 a financial reporter from the *Times* was assigned to investigate.

He decided to begin by making an unannounced, personal inspection of the Westminster-on-Tyne pig farm, which was located, according to the company's letterhead, near the town of Okehampton, in Devon.

He failed to find it. It seemed not to be there. Residents of the area were willing to help, but had frankly never heard of the Westminster-on-Tyne Livestock Company. Just the smell alone should have made the search less difficult, and this reasoning was applied, but all physical and olfactory traces remained elusive.

Now, an investigative reporter and a good bloodhound have much in common, and the *Times* reporter demonstrated this by shrewdly dropping anchor in a pub very near the Okehampton post office. Many pints later, a servant of Her Majesty's Royal Mail was induced to suspend his customers' right to privacy just long enough to divulge that all mail addressed to the Westminster-on-Tyne Livestock Company was routinely delivered to the Okehampton residence of a cab-driver named Charlie.

And that's where the *Times* reporter finally found the most modern pig farm in all of Europe. It was located in Charlie Burlington's very small back yard – a marvel of agricultural miniaturization and a model for every time-and-motion expert. For, instead of struggling with the fuss and mess and expense, not to mention the residential zoning bylaws, of a twelve-thousand-pig porkery, Charlie had simply purchased one pig – a single sow – and sold her 11,972 times. She had also been photographed 11,972 times – or rather, a dozen of her photographic poses had been duplicated in that quantity – for distribution to her 11,972 proud owners.

That she was a decidedly photogenic specimen was attested to by the full-page spread she was given in a subsequent *Times*

weekend supplement. Whether or not this adequately compen-
sated for the fact that she had proven infertile – probably to
Charlie Burlington's great relief – might have remained a moot
point if Charlie's investors had been content to leave it so.

But they weren't. Charlie was seized by the local constabu-
lary and hauled into court to answer charges of impersonating a
pig breeder. The presiding magistrate took a dim view of such
behaviour, and especially of Charlie's claim – undeniably made
in the classified-ad section of fourteen British newspapers – that
the tumbledown doghouse in his back yard and the single battered pail he used to feed his pig-of-11,972-names constituted
Europe's most technologically advanced pig farm. Such exag-
geration, while doubtless modern in its irresponsibility, was an
intolerable insult to all true farmers and upstanding Englishmen.
Charlie was sentenced to four years in prison and ordered to
return whatever monies remained from his ill-advised venture.

According to straightforward, working-class mathematics,
that should have been $2,999,800 – i.e., $3 million minus the
cost of a single sow. But somehow Charlie had miniaturized this
part of his operation, too. Though he had acquired no obvious
new assets, nor suddenly begun to spend money like there was
no tomorrow, the court's trustee was unable to find more than
half a million dollars in the account of the Westminster-on-
Tyne Livestock Company.

British pork, they say, has always been well received in
Switzerland.

Bogus Birdman
of Bronxville

The Escapades of Paperhanger Frank Abagnale, Jr.

Frank Abagnale, Jr., had a problem. At the age of only fifteen he was already six feet tall, weighed 170 pounds, and looked twice his age, in a disarming, boyish sort of way. Women couldn't seem to keep their hands off him. Frank couldn't seem to keep his hands off women. It cost him a lot of time and money.

It wasn't long before Frank Abagnale had two problems. His parents, who had always paid his bills, divorced, and the family's home was sold. Frank decided to stick with his father. He registered in a new school and got a job at a Bronx warehouse on the side.

His father, intent on encouraging such enterprise, gave Frank his own Mobil Oil card. It didn't take Frank long to learn that you can buy a lot more with a Mobil Oil card than just oil.

Seventeen thousand dollars'* worth of charges later, Frank had himself a third problem.

At this point, he left home. It was 1964; he had the clothes on his back and a thousand dollars in his bank account. He passed himself off as twenty-six years old and got a job as a truck driver's helper. The pay was fourteen dollars an hour, but he soon had a bevy of female friends who cost a lot more than that. Frank began to write a lot of cheques against his thousand-dollar bank account.

It wasn't long before Frank had himself a fourth problem.

Writing rubber cheques is not considered particularly high-rent by the crime fraternity. It suggests a lack of long-term vision. There's no future in it. As a crook, Frank would always suffer from this lack of foresight. But he was resourceful, and he had an undeniable ability to make the best of the moment. One of those moments came as he was walking down New York's Forty-second Street, past the Commodore Hotel.

As he passed the revolving hotel door, it disgorged an Eastern Airlines flight crew, complete with pilot, co-pilot, navigator, and four stewardesses. They were all laughing, resplendent in their dashing airline uniforms.

Now, Frank had a particular thing for airline stewardesses. He'd already experienced several, and they'd made quite an impression on him. But he also noted the deference of the doorman to the pilots. It occurred to him that pilots probably had access to more of this world's pleasures than most other men – not the least of which was being able to cash a bum cheque almost anywhere without hassle.

---

* For consistency, all dollar amounts in this volume have been adjusted to 1990 values.

So Frank Abagnale decided to become a pilot. Not a real pilot, of course; he was far too impatient for that. A fake pilot would do. He called up Pan American Airlines' purchasing department and explained that he was a Los Angeles-based Pan Am co-pilot due out on a return flight that evening, but that his uniform had been lost by the hotel cleaners. Could he be supplied with a replacement?

To his astonishment, he could. He was given the address of Pan Am's New York tailor and told to present himself for an appointment in an hour. At Well-Built Tailors, an obliging clerk fitted him with a co-pilot's uniform and a visored cap. The "hardware" (Pan Am's emblem and wings) would be issued to him by Pan Am's commissary, at Kennedy Airport.

With more gall than brains, Abagnale brazened his way past the commissary's guard and located the door to Pan Am's stores. Once again, an obliging clerk filled his request without verification or suspicion. Once again, Abagnale signed for his contraband with a phoney name and an invented employee number. Nobody even blinked.

His mojo clearly working, Abagnale now called Pan Am operations, identified himself as a teenage reporter researching a story on pilots' lives for his high-school newspaper, and asked if he might interview a Pan Am pilot. No problem. Abagnale grilled an obliging captain for nearly an hour and discovered a great deal about life at thirty-five thousand feet. Of most immediate interest was the fact that every Pan Am pilot needed a pilot's licence and a Pan Am ID card, that Pan Am operated out of five U.S. bases (which didn't include Los Angeles), and that members of the flight crews of any International Air Transport Authority-member airline could fly on any other airline for free, simply by filling out a "deadheading" request.

Deadheading. It had an ominous ring to it, but Abagnale

immediately recognized its extraordinary potential for an ambitious paperhanger. True, he didn't have a clue what a pilot's licence or a Pan Am ID card looked like, but such problems evaporate rapidly when attacked with the blind optimism of the tall-but-very-young.

Abagnale borrowed a business suit, located an ID company in the yellow pages, introduced himself as a representative of Carib Air, and asked for some sample cards. The salesman was happy to oblige. Abagnale suggested they mock one up to see what it would look like in final form. The salesman obliged again. He took Abagnale's picture and plasticized the sample. Excellent. Now all Abagnale needed was the official Pan Am logo, and he solved that problem by using the Pan Am decal out of a $10.49 Pan Am model-airplane kit. It looked indistinguishable from the real thing, and it adhered to the plastic as though it had been embossed. His official Pan Am identification was now complete.

The pilot's licence presented a trickier challenge; they don't just hand out samples in stationery stores. But, after several weeks of foraging in libraries and bookstores, Abagnale found the solution in the back of a flying magazine. A Milwaukee company offered to engrave a large-scale duplicate pilot's licence in silver, mounted on a hardwood plaque, for $175. All the pilot had to do was mail in his name, birthdate, social-security number, FAA licence number, ratings, and an address.

Abagnale did that, inventing all the numbers and giving himself an air-transport rating suitable for flying commercial jets. The company obliged. When the plaque arrived, Abagnale took it to a local printer, who also obliged: in half an hour the plaque had been photographed, reduced, and printed onto heavy white stock. Frank Abagnale was now cleared to fly the friendly skies as an airline pilot.

He began with a few dry runs at ground level. It didn't take long to discover that his suspicions on that fateful day in front of the Commodore Hotel had been right on the money. The whole world bows before a splendid uniform. People smiled and co-operated. Men admired and envied. Women approved and often became extraordinarily obliging. And the best thing of all: bank tellers, airline clerks, store proprietors, travel agents, and restaurant owners were suddenly delighted to cash his cheques.

Yes, it was low-grade crime, it left a dangerous paper trail, but its detractors had obviously never envisioned a paperhanging operation backed by the resources of one of the world's premier airlines. Within days, Abagnale was awash in money. He wore out several dozen aliases. He opened and overdrew more accounts than a Swiss banking operation. He cashed cheques in so many places that he eventually exhausted whole sections of New York. And, when he'd harvested the city about as thoroughly as he dared, he dry-cleaned the uniform, polished up his Pan Am ID and pilot's licence, and took to the skies.

It was here that his paperhanging operation really gained altitude. By now comfortably conversant with airline procedures and airline jargon – he'd spent several months hanging around La Guardia's bars with pilots and stewardesses – he began to deadhead into cities all over the United States. It was just as he'd fantasized. Each new airport, each new city proved yet another bonanza of cheque-cashing opportunities. Where he had previously harvested mere thousands, he now harvested tens of thousands. In his first year of deadheading he fleeced over two hundred American cities and airports. Then he expanded into Europe.

If being a pilot on the ground had been satisfying, being one in the air proved downright exhilarating. Abagnale's social life, never particularly slow, really hit cruising speed. He discovered that flight crews, always on the move, lived a twenty-four-hour life. Since their schedules worked against the more normal dawn-to-dusk relationships of the earthbound, many resorted to living like permanent tourists, partying at the drop of a hat and at the most unlikely hours. A party might start at three o'clock in the morning and last until noon, or begin at three o'clock in the afternoon and end at midnight. People flew in and out of each other's lives as if they were airports, and the resulting chaos proved perfect for an interloping paperhanger always on the move.

And the overhead costs couldn't be beat. With his Pan Am ID and employee number, Abagnale not only flew free but lived free, drove free, ate free, and played free. Pan Am paid for almost everything. All he ever had to do was sign a claims form and help himself. And wherever he went, in restaurants or stores or whenever he checked out of a hotel, he invariably cashed another cheque.

Not that there weren't occasional snags. On his second deadhead flight, the Boeing 707 was full and the stewardess showed him to the jumpseat, a little fold-down ledge right in the cockpit. The pilots quizzed him in comradely fashion about his aviation background and then, to his horror, offered him the jet's controls – a courtesy Abagnale would soon encounter regularly. Within a year he would fly jumpseat often enough to be so familiar with cockpit procedures that he actually would accept a jet's controls for an hour or so on several occasions. On this occasion, fortunately, he was able to sidestep disaster with a wave and a wisecrack. But, before deadheading again, he made sure to concoct a more believable flight-training history.

An even closer brush with disaster occurred in Eureka, California, the day after Abagnale discovered he'd accidentally passed a bum cheque with his real name and father's address scribbled on the back. Hoping against hope that the cheque hadn't yet been processed, he telephoned the manager of the small bank involved to ask whether the cheque had already been received. It certainly had. She had just left a message with the FBI and was impressed at how quickly they were returning her call. Quickly shifting gears, Abagnale acknowledged the compliment, said they'd be sending a man to pick up the cheque within the hour, and sent himself within a few minutes. When the real FBI arrived later that afternoon, the incriminating cheque and its endorser were already four thousand miles away, in Miami.

Life continued in this fashion for almost two years. Abagnale was now rich, but always running. Were all his bouncing cheques simply being noted and ignored in a hundred unconnected police precincts? Or was someone already connecting the individual strings into an inexorably closing net? Had anyone at Pan Am become suspicious yet? How much time was there left before he had to bail out and disappear?

At least part of that question was answered rather dramatically on Friday, November 5, 1966, the day Abagnale decided to deadhead from New Orleans to Miami on National Airlines flight 106. With over two hundred deadhead flights under his belt, jumpseating had become old hat. He greeted the flight crew breezily, plunked himself down behind the First Officer, and began to chat.

The chat was interrupted by a call from the tower.

Abagnale couldn't hear the call, because he hadn't been offered any earphones. But the atmosphere in the cockpit suddenly tensed. The captain turned to Abagnale and gave him a hard, searching look.

"Could I see your Pan Am ID and your pilot's licence, please?

Abagnale tried desperately to look unconcerned. "Of course. Here you are."

The captain took the cards and examined them carefully. He radioed the numbers to the tower and listened for another moment. "Yes. Yes. No, I don't think so. They look okay to me."

When he gave the cards back, he shrugged. "Don't know what that was all about," he said. But the mood didn't really warm up to the usual temperature after that, and, when the DC-8 touched down in Miami, the tower called again. That's when Abagnale knew he was in real trouble. The plane didn't taxi to the gate. It pulled up on the ramp.

When the door opened, two Dade County sheriff's officers blocked the entrance. They took Abagnale into custody and drove him to their downtown office. They ignored his protestations of outrage, but didn't seem to be taking a very personal interest in his case. They locked him in an interrogation room, but didn't interrogate him. It wasn't until a puzzled FBI agent showed up around midnight that Abagnale was able to stitch together what had happened.

The Federal Aviation Authority in New Orleans had called the Miami airport to hold Abagnale. The Miami tower had called the Dade County sheriff's office to do the job, but had not told them on whose behalf. The sheriff's office had assumed the request was FBI, but when no FBI showed up, finally called them at ten o'clock in the evening. Nobody at Miami FBI appeared to know anything about Abagnale, and the length of time he could be held without being charged was running out. Meanwhile, the Miami tower personnel had changed shift, and the sheriff's-office dispatcher had gone home. There was nothing for the FBI to do but apologize to Abagnale and let him go. (Had they searched his flight-bag they would have found over $35,000 in cash and an eyebrow-raising bundle of blank cheques.) By the time FAA officials showed up Monday morning, having discovered in a routine records check that Abagnale had never been issued a legal pilot's licence, he had escaped to Atlanta. And this time, he'd flown as a cash-paying passenger.

That put the deadheading part of Abagnale's paperhanging career into reverse thrust, and might have produced a few second thoughts about the future in anyone over the age of twenty-five – but Abagnale, being barely eighteen, saw the problem largely in terms of scale. Being earthbound again was certainly going to reduce his take, but the real stumbling-block, he decided, was his use of personal cheques. Generally speaking, you couldn't pass a personal cheque for more than a few hundred dollars. People took greater notice and signatures were scrutinized more carefully when you exceeded that amount. What he had to do was find a way to increase the amount by using non-personal cheques or by expanding his banking horizons in some other way. It was simply too early to retire. He had been making plenty of money, but he'd been spending plenty, too – mostly on high living and pliant stewardesses. His stashes were still too few and far between. He couldn't yet afford to hang up that uniform.

So Abagnale began to study banking procedures. As usual, his method was hands-on – he dated bank tellers. His knowledge about bank tellers and cheques soon became encyclopaedic. The former helped when juggling phoney accounts and transfers, where charm and psychology were needed in interchangeable amounts. The latter resulted in yet another evolutionary shift in the art of paperhanging.

Abagnale began to manipulate routing numbers – the numbers printed in computer-readable ink across the bottom of all cheques. Those numbers told a computer, or any bank clerk who knew the code, where and by whom the cheque had been issued, the credit rating of the customer, the clearing house to which the cheque should be sent, the bank against which the cheque had been drawn, the address of that bank, and the customer's account number. All this allowed the bank's computers to process even a very complex cheque in a very short time.

So short, it gave a paperhanger very little time to run.

What attracted Abagnale was the marvellous confusion that occurred when those numbers were mixed up. A cheque with a doctored routing code fell into a computer-generated limbo. Automatically sent to the bank indicated by the code, it was kicked out by the computer because the address didn't match. Assessed by a clerk, it was filed back into the system en route to the bank printed on its face, only to be kicked out again because the bank identification number didn't match. By the time this cheque had been kicked around the system often enough to attract a less-than-routine inspection by a clerk, it had been in limbo for weeks.

And best of all, those magnetic numbers could be purchased in stick-on form at an ordinary craft store.

For Abagnale, the most immediate benefit of this discovery was that he could now hang paper in a given city for weeks – instead of merely days – before having to run. But he soon discovered additional benefits. The machines used by banks to process deposit slips responded to those numbers, too. They were set up to automatically direct funds into a depositor's account, either by reading the routing number – if the customer had supplied it – or, as a default setting, by reading the depositor's name and address. Most customers, Abagnale noticed, never bothered to supply their routing number. Always helpful, Abagnale decided to do this for them. He pocketed a fistful of deposit slips from their trays on the bank's counter, took them home, applied his own number to each slip with magnetic-ink stick-ons, and returned the slips to the bank's counter.

Four days later he returned to the bank and checked his account. Bingo. It had grown from $1,250 to $214,382.25. Abagnale withdrew $200,000, explaining that he was buying a house. But he didn't. He flew to Hawaii with a girlfriend and spent the money on her. He was, after all, just a teenager.

But what finally brought all these ingredients together – magnetic numbers, routing codes, a knowledge of accounts and transfers, and the growing desire to grow beyond the limits of personal cheques – was Abagnale's discovery of the Itek camera and the offset press. An Itek produces an engraving of anything it photographs (i.e., currency bills, blank cheques, or printed forms), which can then be printed onto any weight of paper stock by an offset press.

Abagnale's first opportunity to apply this technology came when a Pan Am stewardess with whom he had just spent an evening studying airline manuals in bed complained that she would now be unable to get her salary cheque cashed at the front desk, since it was after midnight, and her flight left at 5:30 a.m.

Suddenly, every paperhanging instinct in Abagnale's body stood to attention. He quickly, generously, offered to cash the cheque for her. He just happened to have that kind of cash on his person because he'd cashed his own cheque earlier that day. The stewardess, naturally, was only too happy to accept.

It was a move that would net Abagnale, and cost Pan Am, millions.

He now had his mitts on a genuine Pan Am salary cheque, signed and with a legitimate account number. Blanking out the name and the amount was easy. Adjusting the routing code was, too. Photographing and printing it took a little more practice, but it wasn't long before he was turning out very convincing replicas. The mass-production department of Abagnale's paper-hanging operation was fast becoming satisfactorily mechanized. It now occurred to Abagnale that his distribution department was seriously undermanned.

Or underwomanned. The image of a whole bevy of cheque-cashing stewardesses came readily to mind. Abagnale in their midst as their handsome uniformed manager added a certain flair. Combining business with pleasure had always been Abagnale's style. And the risk – well, risk had never been something Abagnale spent much time worrying about.

So he didn't.

Instead, he proceeded to cook up the crowning glory of his Pan Am career.

Using facsimile Pan Am stationery, he wrote to the University of Arizona to ask whether they'd be interested in adding Pan Am to their Career Day agenda. Pan Am, he said, was prepared to interview prospective stewardesses who might be considering a career with the airline.

The university certainly was. Abagnale would be provided with an interview room and the school records of all student applicants. If there was anything else they could do to make his stay more pleasant and productive he had only to ask. As usual, Abagnale was finding the world brimming with obliging and co-operative people. He bundled up a sheaf of Pan Am promotional literature on one of his uniformed sweeps through the Pan Am commissary and sent it to the university via Pan Am's mail room, instructing the clerk to send it air mail.

On Career Day, Abagnale was swamped with young women eager to join Pan Am. He selected the thirty best-looking ones and interviewed them. He weeded out the unduly virtuous, prudish, naive, or religious. He was looking for gullibility, broad-mindedness, a zest for adventure, and a devil-may-care attitude. He had no trouble finding eight young women who fit several of those categories quite decisively.

He explained that, although Pan Am was not prepared to hire them as working stewardesses until their studies were completed, he was authorized to hire eight trainees for a special Pan Am public-relations project. This would involve spending the summer touring Europe's most famous cities, being photographed in Pan Am uniform at many of the destinations to which Pan Am flew. Pan Am was planning a big advertising campaign in the fall, and this was a way of assembling the necessary photographs without pulling working stewardesses off the line during the busiest season of the year.

Did they like the idea? The girls practically flipped. Abagnale's feelings were not dissimilar. During the two months before their departure, he visited the California firm which manufactured Pan Am's stewardess uniforms, presented himself as a representative of Pan Am's PR department with a fake letter of introduction, and ordered a uniform for each girl, complete with monogrammed luggage. The order was accepted without question, and his signature on the invoice took care of the payment. Then he reserved a room for each girl at a luxury hotel near Kennedy Airport, and, dressed in his pilot's uniform, put in a request at Pan Am's operations centre for a crew wagon. Again, nobody blinked. The wagon was waiting at the airport when the girls arrived. The driver didn't even request a signature.

The itinerary for the trip read like a million-dollar circuit of the Western world: London, Paris, Rome, Athens, Geneva, Munich, Berlin, Madrid, Oslo, Copenhagen, Vienna, and more.

Abagnale paid for all the airfares in cash but, beyond that, Pan Am unwittingly obliged. All the hotel rooms, the meals, the ground transportation, even some of the bogus photography sessions, were all put on Pan Am's tab.

The payoff, of course, was the multiplier factor in rubber cheques. Abagnale set a furious pace, moving from hotel to hotel and city to city almost every day – and every day the girls were required to sign off forged expense cheques, drawn on Pan Am in their own names. With the girls strategically assembled before the main desk, Abagnale gathered those cheques and got the hotels to cash them "for the girls." Naturally, he pocketed the cash. (The girls thought these cheques simply covered the cost of meals and accommodation and didn't expect any money from them.) Every two weeks they also signed over their forged salary cheques, which Abagnale cashed in the same way. These, however, he reimbursed to them in cash, instructing them to send their earnings home at regular intervals by money order.

The trickiest part of the operation was avoiding any contact with real Pan Am crews. To ensure this, Abagnale instructed the girls to wear their uniforms only during hotel check-ins, photo sessions, and check-outs, and never during flights. They were cautioned never to divulge their Pan Am connections to any flight crew they might encounter, on the grounds that Pan Am didn't want to cause resentment among its working stewardesses over the special treatment these trainees were getting. The precautions obviously worked, because no Pan Am flight crews ever reported Abagnale's Pan Am harem back to home base.

Singlehandedly managing, chaperoning, sheepdogging, and mother-henning a crew of eight exceedingly pretty, frisky, and unpredictable girls around Europe couldn't have been the easiest job in the world, nor – given Abagnale's track record – the most innocent. Concerning this point he later stoutly protested that his policy was always strictly "celibatarian," and that he always managed to fend off their fervent advances.

Whatever the truth, he obviously didn't let too much get in the way of business. When he wrapped up the tour in Copenhagen at the end of the summer he was $2.5 million richer, and still at liberty. He presented each girl with an armful of roses and put them all on a plane back to Arizona.

He, on the other hand, went to ground in a little town called Montpellier, France, to cool his trail. It was becoming clear to him that he had been pushing his luck well into the red zone. Only Pan Am's astonishingly lax security and operations procedures had so far kept the trap from snapping shut. But even Pan Am had to have some glimmerings by now of the pilot-suited buccaneer who had been plundering its treasury for almost four years. It was even harder to believe that the FBI hadn't set its sights on him yet. Clearly it was time to take a break and plan some strategies for the future, for a new identity, for a new career that didn't have prison at the end of it.

Abagnale was right. As usual, his instincts were spot on the money. But this time he was just a little too late. Four months later a barrage of rifle-waving police officers ambushed him in a Montpellier supermarket, and this time there were no loopholes. The Sûreté de France didn't believe in them.

✦

There was more than a little irony in the details of how Abagnale was caught. He was recognized in a Montpellier shop by an Air France stewardess he had dated several years earlier. Obviously, word of his imposture had begun to spread through airline circles. But it was still a fluke, because Montpellier wasn't anywhere near an airport – one of the main reasons Abagnale had chosen the little town.

His choice, moreover, proved flawed for two reasons. Montpellier was located in France. France, during the 1960s, still boasted one of the Western world's most conservative justice systems. French corrections officials didn't believe in rehabilitation. They believed in old-fashioned punishment. When the French Court of Assizes handed him a one-year prison sentence, Abagnale was pleased at having got off so lightly. He quickly discovered he had very little to be pleased about.

His cell in Perpignan Prison was a stone dungeon measuring five feet by five feet by five feet. It was freezing cold, constantly wet, and had no window and no light. He was thrown into this hole totally naked, with no mattress and no blanket. His diet was mostly dry bread and water. During his entire incarceration in Perpignan he was never once let out for exercise or a wash. When he was finally transferred, about six months later, he had lost over sixty pounds, had double pneumonia, and was on the verge of collapse. The Perpignan warden refused him a doctor.

But there was worse to come.

He was informed that fourteen other governments – Italy, Spain, Turkey, Germany, Sweden, England, the United States, Switzerland, Greece, Denmark, Norway, Egypt, Lebanon, and Cyprus – had already requested his extradition. More were expected. Meanwhile, Sweden was next in line. He was handed over to the Swedes.

That was extraordinarily lucky for Abagnale. At least half of the aforementioned countries subscribed to the same correctional system as France – or worse. In fact it was Abagnale's appalling physical condition that convinced the Swedes to sidestep their normal extradition obligations and deport Abagnale directly to the United States. There, under Rule 20 of the United States Penal Code (the "Grab-Bag Law"), which permitted Abagnale to amalgamate the hundreds of state and federal charges outstanding against him, he eagerly pleaded guilty to "all crimes known and unknown" that he had committed in the United States during the past five years.

For his thefts – which were estimated to total over $15 million worldwide – he was sentenced to serve twelve years in the federal penitentiary at Petersburg, Virginia.

When he was paroled after four years, Abagnale was still only twenty-six years old. It took him two more years to find his feet and his métier. As usual, he made the best of the available opportunities.

What he did was to use his manifest skills and experience to become one of America's most popular consultants on white-collar crime. He now lectures throughout North America to the managers of banks, hotels, restaurants, and airlines.

And what he tells them – for very fat fees – is exactly how to defend themselves against people like himself.

Oil's Well
That Ends Well

———◆◆◆———

The Spectacular Home-Stake Oil Swindle

In mid-February 1971, investors in a variety of oil-drilling ventures managed by the widely respected Oklahoma firm of Home-Stake Production Company, received an unexpected jolt.

The U.S. Securities and Exchange Commission charged Home-Stake with selling units of its 1970 drilling venture under false pretences. It contended that Home-Stake had knowingly made seriously inflated claims for the amount of proven oil in that undertaking. As a result, the SEC obliged Home-Stake to offer full refunds to all its investors who wished, in light of this information, to pull out of this venture.

Of Home-Stake's total number of investors, only 890 were directly affected. But thousands of others, many of whom had been investing in Home-Stake since its inception in 1955, suddenly had cause to worry about the security of their other Home-Stake investments.

The names on the roster of Home-Stake investors made up no ordinary list. Home-Stake's ventures were tax shelters, affordable only to the rich. Its investors included many of those who were, or would become, America's best-known lawyers, business tycoons, politicians, and Hollywood entertainers. Entertainers like Jack Benny, Candice Bergen, Alan Alda, and Bob Dylan. Lawyers like Robert B. Fiske, William A. Shea, Richard Storrs, and Thomas E. Dewey. Politicians like senators Jacob K. Javits, Ernest F. Hollings, and Claude R. Kirk. Businessmen like PepsiCo chairman Donald M. Kendall, Western Union chairman R. W. McFall, and NCR Corp. chairman Robert S. Oelman. Plus no fewer than thirty-five General Electric vice-presidents and managers.

The man who ran Home-Stake, and who immediately began crisscrossing the country to calm his investors' fears, was a quiet, confidence-inspiring Oklahoma lawyer named Robert S. Trippet. Son of a bank president, and son-in-law to one of Oklahoma's most successful oil barons, Trippet had a good reputation, was superbly connected, and wealthy in his own right. It seemed impossible that a man of his qualities had intentionally lied to his investors about something as important as a drilling venture's proven oil reserves.

And indeed, Trippet categorically denied that he had done any such thing. The SEC engineers were notorious for their doubts and suspicions, he said. That was understandable; it was their job to keep a tight rein on America's free-wheeling oil companies. But Home-Stake had – and Trippet circulated – two independent engineering surveys confirming the plausibility of Home-Stake's claims. It was true that Home-Stake had had some problems with one of its California oilfields, where the oil was laced with a fine sand difficult to filter out by conventional means. But potential solutions were already being tested. Investors could rest assured that Home-Stake remained one of the most successful, efficiently run oil companies in the country.

On the other hand – and here Trippet dropped his feisty stance – there was nothing worse, from a CEO's standpoint, than running a company backed by unhappy investors. It didn't matter whether they were right or wrong. The relationship had not only to *be* right, but to *feel* right. Therefore he urged one and all, anyone who was the least bit unhappy, doubtful, or dissatisfied with his relationship to Home-Stake, to return his investment contract for a prompt and full refund. No questions asked. No explanation required. In fact, if for any reason any investor wanted out of any of the company's sixteen *other* ventures – not just the 1970 venture the SEC had singled out – Home-Stake was willing to buy back at least a portion of those as well.

That's how important a happy company–investor relationship was considered at Home-Stake.

The speech, the offer, and the sentiment went over well. Trippet had always struck people as flexible and fair. And how could he possibly make such an offer if the company's operations and prospects weren't in as sound a fiscal shape as he said they were?

In the end, only 119 investors, representing less than $25 million of the $115 million* Trippet had raised before the SEC's intervention, decided to withdraw their money.

The rest joined the thousands of other wealthy suckers who

---

* For consistency, all dollar amounts in this volume have been adjusted to 1990 values.

had once again misjudged Trippet's character as thoroughly as Samson had misjudged Delilah.

◆

When Trippet founded the Home-Stake Production Company in 1955, the name already enjoyed an excellent pedigree. It had been part of his wife Helen's family for generations. Her grandfather had founded Home-Stake Oil and Gas in 1917, and her father had founded the Home-Stake Royalty Corporation in 1929. Both companies had, and continue to have, first-class reputations. Trippet gained access to that reputation and its associated clientele by involving Helen's brother, Strother Simpson, in the founding of his company. By the time Strother discovered that Trippet's business ethics were a lot more flexible than those of his forefathers, it was too late to do anything about the name. Simpson and most of the other directors resigned and left the company to Trippet.

In 1955, oil-drilling investment tax shelters were still a fairly new commodity in the United States. To promote American self-sufficiency in oil, the U.S. government had passed a law allowing U.S. investors a 100-per-cent tax write-off on all monies invested in oil drilling or oil production. For anyone in America's top tax bracket in those days, the tax savings were enormous.

It worked this way: A well-heeled lawyer or executive with a taxable income of $1,000,000 faced a tax bill of around $500,000. But if he invested $500,000 in oil production, that entire investment was deductible from his taxable income. Result: a tax bill of only $200,000. Tax savings: $300,000. In effect, the lawyer was investing in an oil-drilling program using $300,000 of the government's money, and only $200,000 of his own. And the best part was, the government's contribution didn't have to be repaid.

From Trippet's perspective, this arrangement had two important advantages. First: the investor got an immediate rush of satisfaction from having legally recaptured $300,000 from the clutches of the IRS. Second: already being, in effect, $300,000 ahead, the investor didn't tend to be as fussy about the size of the eventual return on his investment.

Not that Trippet didn't promise fat returns. He promised plenty: a profit of 400 per cent or better. But since oil properties took years to develop, the returns would be spread over a twelve-year period. In the first years, while the wells were being drilled, returns would be negligible. During years four to eight, when the wells came into full production, the returns would be enormous.

A $500,000 investment, for example, would pay no returns at all in the first year, only $11,250 in the second year, and only $37,500 in the third. But in the fourth year, it would pay a very respectable $140,000; in the fifth, a substantial $350,000; in the sixth, a spectacular $700,000. After that, the returns would drop off again, as the wells became depleted. But the total twelve-year return on that initial $500,000 investment would be about $1.95 million, *plus* the original $300,000 tax deduction. Total return: $2.25 million.

It all sounded very plausible and attractive and safe.

✦

Trippet's first and most important advantage in the investment structure he'd designed was time.

Four years of time. He had four years, from 1955 to 1959, before his first year's investors would be expecting returns of any significance – four years during which the amount of money coming in would significantly exceed the amount of money going out. And even after that, each year's new batch of investors would tend to offset the rising payout of returns his older investors had been led to expect.

Trippet didn't waste any time. He quickly set up, in his own name, an array of service companies to conduct many of the operations normally associated with an oil-production venture.

One company sold engineering studies and surveys to Home-Stake. Another sold it construction materials. A third sold it drilling and earthmoving equipment. A fourth sold it oil-recovery and drilling services. A fifth sold it oil properties and oil leases.

The only problem was that most of these companies existed only on paper. The services and equipment they sold to Home-Stake were mostly invented. Those few companies that actually existed in the real world were generally underequipped and understaffed, their billings wildly exceeding actual services rendered.

And those billings, of course, all ended up in Trippet's pocket.

To maintain appearances, Trippet did buy a few marginal oil properties on which he actually drilled a few wells. But appearance was all he was really interested in. A favourite gimmick was to buy a few cheap acres *just outside* somebody else's derrick-covered oilfield, rig up some dummy derricks with HOME-STAKE prominently emblazoned on them, then photograph the scene to make it look as if the entire field was a Home-Stake enterprise. In what quickly became the norm at Home-Stake Production, the action in its annual report and its promotional brochures was far more dramatic than anything going on in its field operations.

Another trick was to fly investors in to such fields for an inspection tour and photograph them with a Home-Stake derrick grandly gushing oil in the background. (A device known as a "squirter" was routinely bolted onto the wellhead for this effect.) Sometimes the oil was actually oil, but more often it was just cheap kerosene distillate, which was pumped through the wellhead from a tank buried beneath the derrick.

Over the years, Treppit also came up with a number of inspired concepts to pump up the sales of Home-Stake ventures. The most successful was the concept of steamflooding for "secondary oil recovery." This technique was based on the fact that early oil-extraction technologies had been so crude that many "depleted" oilfields still contained as much as 30 per cent of their original oil in the ground. More recently, some oil companies had begun pumping steam or water into such fields, to force up the remaining oil.

The method was custom-made for Treppit, because it made such obvious economic sense. Most people knew that real oil exploration was a highly risky, often-unsuccessful enterprise. Anyone offering a virtually assured 400-per-cent return on such exploration would have been laughed out of the Oil Exchange. But secondary recovery was something else. It was the closest there was in the oil industry to a "no muss, no fuss, no risk" operation. The oil was demonstrably there, and sometimes the old holes were even reusable. The properties were cheap, the overhead low, and the returns self-evidently less speculative. The concept proved so successful in lowering the anxiety level and scepticism of thousands of potential Home-Stake investors that Treppit committed a large percentage of Home-Stake's production programs to steamflooding.

The only kicker was: it didn't work. Not very well, at any rate. Standard Oil of California had tried it and finally given up.

So had Texaco. Some oil was always recovered, but rarely enough to justify the investment. It was a concept that was still awaiting the right technology.

In the meantime, however, it had great promotional value. Treppit scouted around until he found a huge dryland farm in southern California that was watered by an enormous irrigation system. He convinced the owner to "rent" this system to Home-Stake for a brief photo opportunity. Painting the pipes bright pink, he marked some with a large "O" and others with a large "X." He also plastered prominent HOME-STAKE signs on every available surface. The effect, particularly from the air, gave the appearance of a huge secondary-oil-recovery facility, with the X-pipes signifying production wells and the O-pipes feeding steam-injection sites. Once again, for Robert Treppit, the photograph proved more profitable than the drilling rig.

◆

Until 1959, the care and feeding of Home-Stake's investors was a cakewalk. With none of them expecting anything, such expectations were easy to meet and even exceed. Treppit sent them all glossy quarterly brochures with the impressive photos already described. He gave them upbeat reports and vague-but-optimistic-sounding forecasts. And, just to put everyone in the most receptive frame of mind, he always slightly exceeded the amount of the small initial payments scheduled to be paid out for the first three years. This didn't cost him much, and it gave his reports and predictions an extra patina of credibility.

Such moves paid off. In both the second and the third years (1957 and 1958), many initial investors signed up for additional ventures – or their business manager signed them up. Phyllis Diller climbed aboard. So did Buddy Hackett. Liza Minnelli.

Sandy Duncan. Treppit sold over $10 million worth of invest-
ments in those two years.

By year four, of course, the balance began to shift. Now
people began to expect some real money. In anticipation of this,
Treppit announced his first small problems with production –
sand in the oil, bad weather, union troubles – the sorts of problems reasonable people would understand and tolerate. The
payouts that year were lower than expected, but not so low as to
produce investor revolt. The few who complained found Treppit
congenial and willing to buy them out.

The plan kept working. Word about Home-Stake got
around. By 1962 Treppit was pulling in over $15 million in
investments from New York alone. The payouts kept being
lower than forecast, for reasons both understandable and
unavoidable, but the fact that Treppit was always prepared to buy
out unhappy investors meant that few actually requested it. After
all, they were still ahead by the amount of their initial tax
savings, and that thought always cushioned any disappointment
over lower returns. So Home-Stake's investor list continued to
grow in both quantity and quality. Faye Dunaway and Mike
Nichols signed up. So did Buffy Sainte-Marie and Tony Curtis.
Bob Dylan bought additional units. Dozens of company presidents and chairmen added a Wall Street seal of approval. Treppit
was now spending half his time schmoozing the rich and
famous in New York and California, and he was good at it –
careful never to hard-sell, listening more than talking, making a
point of remembering people's names and faces.

With all that PR, nobody seemed to notice the more ominous
signs.

The fact, for example, that, during its first seven years of
operation, Home-Stake had used no fewer than five different

accounting firms, most of whom had quietly quit after just one year rather than go head-to-head with Treppit over the irregularities and illegalities they were discovering in Home-Stake's books.

The fact that Home-Stake often sold more investments in a given year than its prospectuses acknowledged, which, unbeknownst to its investors, significantly reduced the value of their individual investments.

The fact that Home-Stake, ostensibly an oil-producing company, was hardly producing any oil.

Some years Treppit couldn't even convince his current accounting firm to sign Home-Stake's annual report. In such cases, Treppit just signed it himself.

Nobody seemed to notice – or care.

All this might have gone on indefinitely, and may have been exactly what Treppit had originally had in mind. Such operations are called Ponzi schemes, after the Boston swindler Charles Ponzi, who in the 1920s concocted a pyramid-investment system that, while pretending to be a productive, profitable business, did nothing but pay early investors with the contributions of later investors, hoping that incoming contributions would always exceed outgoing payments. While they did, for several frantic months, Ponzi made spectacular profits and was able to siphon off millions. But when somebody figured it out and blew the whistle, the scheme instantly collapsed. The whistle-blower has always been the Achilles' heel of a Ponzi scheme.

By 1967, despite all of Treppit's PR and goodwill, there were a number of potential whistle-blowers among Home-Stake's investors, and they were starting to give Treppit a hard time. They didn't want to be bought out and they didn't want to be schmoozed. They just wanted their 400-per-cent returns. And since they were often very powerful men – business tycoons, prominent lawyers, or judges – they were not to be trifled with.

This led Treppit to establish his infamous multi-tiered payment system. Investors began to be assigned to one of three categories: "A" (powerful, well-connected, and immune to cajolery), "B" (powerful or well-connected, but willing to sit still for a good sob story), and "C" (not influential or aggressive enough to worry about).

The investors in the "A" category got their 400-per-cent returns and a lot of thank-you-very-much. Investors in the "B" category were regaled with excuses and a variety of lower payments, but were monitored to ensure they weren't pushed beyond their limits. Investors in the "C" category were regaled with excuses and lots of friendly mail, but no money at all, and were ignored when they complained or protested.

Once again, this ruse paid off. It cost Treppit a little more in the short run, but most of those company presidents, lawyers, and judges, pleased with their 400-per-cent returns, influenced a lot of their associates to sign up. "B"-category investors required a lot more mail, chit-chat, and constantly adjusted payments, but they proved surprisingly susceptible to this treatment and generally signed up for additional ventures when they felt flush. And the "C" category – well, they didn't matter much, anyway. Their investments were usually the smallest and their influence insufficient to cause Home-Stake much trouble.

Then there was luck, plain dumb luck. Treppit had his share of that, too. The years 1968 and 1969 turned out to be boom times in the stock market, and many investors found themselves awash in money they wanted to shield from the IRS. With its twelve-year history, Home-Stake was perfectly positioned to absorb that cash. Its annual take rose to $85 million in 1968 and $100 million in 1969 – so much money that Treppit was able to slash Home-Stake's already-minimal oil activity by almost half again. By now, Home-Stake was making so little money from oil that its accountants were warning Treppit he would lose his tax-shelter status if the IRS ever found out. It was taking more and more outrageous bookkeeping to fudge the real source of Home-Stake's "profits."

But Treppit refused to be cowed by government agents or bureaucrats. He'd already had a couple of dust-ups with the IRS and the SEC, and he'd always managed to outmanoeuvre them. All that had ever resulted was a slap on the wrist and a demand that he promise not to do something or other again. He had always been able to see these guys coming.

When the stock market finally corrected in 1970 and everybody lost a bundle, the goodwill of Treppit's investors diminished sharply. For a while, the good ship Home-Stake tossed in dangerous waters. But at the last minute Treppit devised another cunning ploy that not only rescued the company but did so at IRS expense. He offered Home-Stake complainers the option of donating their Home-Stake ventures to charity.

Put baldly that way, it didn't sound very inspired. But Treppit had arranged to provide his investors with certain inducements. These were official evaluations, provided by one of Home-Stake's infinitely malleable engineering firms, of the ostensible market value of Home-Stake's ventures. Needless to say, these values were enormously inflated. So Home-Stake investors could dump their disappointing investments on their favourite charities for yet another large tax deduction. Combined with the original tax saving in the original first year of purchase, the result was often as close to their originally expected 400-per-cent return as they could possibly have hoped for.

It was another inspired deception, and thousands of Home-Stake investors took advantage of it. Most of them probably didn't even realize it *was* a deception. For them – especially those who had been invested in Home-Stake for many years – it was simply an easy, non-confrontational way to get out of what had become an increasingly disappointing investment.

American charities thus became one of the largest groups of investors in Home-Stake ventures. They were, needless to say, consigned by Treppit to category "C."

Freed of a wave of potential whistle-blowers, Treppit became increasingly brash about helping himself to his company's assets. Not content with such annual ruses as having Home-Stake pay his paper companies Rolls-Royce prices for Volkswagen properties, he now invoked what he and a close associate laughingly called their "Great Train Robbery." It involved having Home-Stake buy back a kind of stock option Trippet had written into his management contract with the company back in 1955. It wasn't really a stock option, but it had a similar effect – Trippet called it a "reversionary interest" – and it guaranteed him 10 per cent of the profits from any oil-production venture that continued to make money after its twelve-year paper life had expired. Now this was all nonsense – Home-Stake had never produced enough oil to make a legitimate profit in any of its ventures – but Treppit had one of his engineering firms draw up an estimate of what 10 per cent of such profits *might be in the future* and came up with an amount of $12.5 million. That's what he now obliged Home-Stake, through a devious and complex set of financial manoeuvrings, to pay him in cash.

Not surprisingly, this resulted in yet another abrupt resignation of Home-Stake's accounting firm of the day, and even the departure of several of its previously pliable directors. Nobody wanted to go to jail that badly. But Treppit brazened it out and simply got himself another accountant – one that was willing to let Home-Stake do its own accounting and just sign whatever papers Treppit shoved under his nose.

✦

If Treppit had scaled down his relentless fleecing of Home-Stake's cash reserves, if he'd stopped playing so fast and loose with accounting principles, if he'd eased off on his reckless flouting of SEC and IRS regulations, he might have been able to keep this scam going for many more years. But by 1971 the combination of all these problems, plus the inevitable rumours that accompanied them, and the damaging press stories that resulted, caused the first serious loss of momentum Home-Stake had experienced in fifteen years. That year, the company missed its $125-million target by over $50 million. The loss proved symptomatic of larger problems. Some investors had compared notes and had discovered they'd been paid different rates of return for identical investments. Lawsuits and formal complaints to a wide variety of state and federal agencies began sprouting all over the place. The IRS began a major investigation. The SEC finally woke up and decided to take a closer look at this company that so many people were increasingly unhappy about.

The SEC didn't like what it saw. Its first move was to order the already-described refund offer to participants in Home-Stake's 1970s venture, an order SEC officials frankly hoped would put Home-Stake out of business, but which Treppit managed largely to thwart. But its second move proved harder to sidestep. In 1972, after further investigation, the SEC subpoenaed every officer of Home-Stake's board and management, and proceeded with a dragnet examination of all of Home-Stake's books and records.

That's when the rubber finally hit the road.

It didn't take long for the SEC's financial gumshoes to discover Treppit's amazing list of transgressions: his dummy companies; his wide-ranging use of Home-Stake funds for his own purposes; his Ponzi-like business methods; and the company's steadily diminishing oil production over the years.

But they also discovered that Treppit had once again anticipated them. The company didn't belong to him any more. It had been hastily "made available" to a notorious New Mexico entrepreneur by the name of E. M. Riebold, who had quickly stacked Home-Stake's board of directors and transferred the bulk of Home-Stake's cash reserves into his own deeply indebted New Mexico companies.

Treppit's purpose in letting this happen had been to dump the responsibility for Home-Stake's management into the hands of people who were prepared to remain uninformed about his company's past. Riebold's purpose in accepting this arrangement had been to get his mitts on some desperately needed cash. When the SEC officials showed up, Home-Stake was on the verge of being transferred from Tulsa to New Denver.

The SEC promptly ordered a reversal of all those transactions.

Treppit and twelve of his Home-Stake officers were indicted on charges of conspiring to defraud thousands of Home-Stake investors by conducting a Ponzi-type swindle for the purpose of stealing their investment contributions.

Home-Stake Production was put into the hands of a government trustee, who pronounced it officially insolvent.

✦

Press reaction, when the Home-Stake story hit the streets, was swift, detailed, and not particularly sympathetic. The *Wall Street Journal* led off with an article headlined "The Big Write-Off: Rich Investors' Losses in New Ponzi Scheme Could Hit 500 Million." *Time* magazine ran a story entitled "Gulling the Beautiful People"; *Newsweek* called it "The Star-Spangled Swindle." All over Europe and North America, reporters found it hard not to gloat over the extent to which America's upper crust, advised by America's highest-priced accountants and investment consultants, had been conned and suckered like any ordinary Joe.

Meanwhile, if the SEC had thought its takeover of Home-Stake's affairs would bring anything to a standstill, it was badly mistaken. Relieved of their responsibility to run a company, Home-Stake's officers promptly headed for the courts and began to counter-sue. A deluge of suits and counter-suits swept through the Los Angeles law courts. Investors, both individually and in groups, sued the company and the company's officers. The company's officers counter-sued the groups in an effort to block them. The officers sued each other and the SEC sued them.

On the face of it, things looked disastrous for Home-Stake's officers – especially for Treppit. He'd left a paper trail as wide as a yellow brick road, and it all showed very plainly where theft and fraud had occurred. A private detective testified that Treppit had tried to get him to crack Home-Stake's new locks shortly after the SEC's takeover; Treppit had clearly wanted to remove a lot of files he hadn't had a chance to remove earlier. But the detective had thought better of it, and turned Treppit down.

Still, this was a business trial, and a very complex one at that. It didn't take Treppit long to realize that his best defence lay in making it even more complex – as long, complex, and confusing as he possibly could.

Treppit rented himself an office, hired himself a lawyer, and began to obfuscate.

By the time the case came to trial, four years later, it had become one of the largest, most complex fraud cases in American history. With seven defendants, dozens of lawyers, and millions of pages of evidence and submissions – Treppit had been very busy – it would have taken a judge with near-clairvoyance in the areas of business, law, psychology, and oil production to make sense of it all.

The prosecution didn't get such a judge. In fact, the defendants were successful in having the case moved from Los Angeles – where such a judge might have existed – to Tulsa, Oklahoma, where Judge Allen E. Barrow had little patience with "rich eastern fancypants lawyers" and never did manage to grasp what the financial issues were all about. When it came to investments, he felt, it was buyer beware; what more was there to understand? What was important to him was that he knew most of the defendants – or their lawyers – personally and they were his kind of people.

One after another, the defendants were let off the hook. Some were found not guilty. Some were given small fines and unsupervised probation. Some were given probation and no fines at all.

As for Treppit, his transgressions had been so flagrant, numerous, and large, and his indictment so serious – twenty-two counts of securities fraud, twelve counts of income-tax fraud, and three counts of mail fraud – that even Judge Barrow couldn't let him off entirely. Ignoring the prosecution's demand for a fifty-year prison term, he permitted Treppit to plea-bargain a deal whereby Treppit agreed to change his plea from "not guilty" to "no contest" (a fancy way of legally admitting guilt without admitting guilt) in exchange for a $19,000 fine and no prison term at all.

In the Tulsa County Jail, where Treppit was held for twenty-five hours while awaiting sentencing – the sum total of his prison experience – one of the inmates asked him: "How in hell did you steal $200 million? I broke my ass stealing $200 and I'll probably be in here forever."

"If you give back the $200 million, they'll probably go easier on you," another prisoner advised.

"Give it back, shit. They'll be a few months in jail, then get out and start spending it," the first inmate snorted.[*]

As the *Tulsa Tribune*'s lead editorial put it the following day: "On Tuesday, U.S. District Judge Allen E. Barrow of Tulsa seemed to have accomplished the difficult feat of topping himself in the matter of trivial sentences."

✦

Ironically, when all was said and done, the greatest punishment was reserved for the victims.

Not only had they lost a total of $700 million in original investments, plus another $1.7 billion in lost returns on those investments, they now had to face the results of an exhaustive IRS investigation of Home-Stake's operations.

The first, most obvious finding was that Home-Stake had never produced enough oil to justify its tax-shelter status. This

---

[*] As quoted in *Stealing from the Rich* by David McClintick. See "Sources."

meant that all deductions based on the IRS ruling about oil-production tax shelters were pronounced null and void.

Result: most Home-Stake investors now faced an IRS bill for huge amounts of back taxes, based on these denied deductions.

But there was worse to come. The donations to charity, based on market evaluations provided by Home-Stake's engineers, were also examined and deemed fraudulent. They too were denied, and bills for back taxes were sent to all investors who had donated their ventures to charities.

Worse yet – and here the IRS proved itself a truly pitiless bean-counter – there were now fines to be paid for the "late payment" of all these back taxes. Most payments, of course, were by now many years "late." And the fines levied on them were calculated at compounded rates.

So, a corporate president who, over Home-Stake's eighteen years of operation, might have invested a total of $2.5 million in Home-Stake ventures (not an uncommon example) now faced a repayment of 60 per cent in denied deductions ($1.5 million) plus $2 million in compounded fines, for a bruising tax bill of $3.5 million. And if he'd donated his ventures to charity, as many of them had, the damages could go as high as $6 million.

As one journalist put it: "If these guys hadn't already suffered heart attacks from forty years at General Electric, this sure as hell was guaranteed to do the job."

In fact, the total cost to U.S. taxpayers for the Home-Stake swindle – including lost investments, lost interest, lost earnings, unpaid taxes, and the staggering cost of four years of court and legal proceedings – added up to $6.5 billion.

Will that be cash, or charge?

The Pharaoh of
Pyramid Selling

*The Inspirational Multiplication
Methods of Glenn Wesley Turner*

When Glenn Turner left his birthplace of Marion, South Carolina, at the age of thirty-one, he was already an accomplished salesman.

He had a comfortable white brick house on Main Street to prove it. He had a wife and three sons. He was earning a whopping $200,000 a year selling electric sewing machines. He was so good at it that he'd once sold a machine to a woman whose nearest access to electricity was a friend's house two miles down the road.

Everybody said he could talk the hind legs off a mule.

A local television show had featured Turner as the county's "Cinderella Story" of the decade.

And yet, in 1966, he sold his sewing-machine franchise to a partner for a dollar and packed up for Florida.

He had just discovered the truly inspirational multiplying characteristics of the common housefly.

✦

It was a salesman for the cosmetics firm Holiday Magic who'd shown Turner the numbers.

Two houseflies, in a single copulation, produced 200 houseflies.

Left to their own devices, these 200 flies produced, in another single copulation, 40,000 more flies. These in turn produced 8,000,000 flies.

Not bad. But now the numbers really started to cook. The next copulation produced a whopping 1.6 billion. The next, 320 billion. The next, an incomprehensible 64 trillion.

There wasn't even a name in the dictionary for how many the copulation after that produced.

Glenn Turner found those numbers extraordinarily fascinating – especially when the Holiday Magic salesman put a dollar sign in front of them, and proceeded to tell Turner all about the truly inspirational multiplying characteristics of something called "pyramid selling."

The system was as simple as its numbers were devastating. It worked like a chain letter. You convinced 12 salesmen to fork over ("invest") $25,000 each for the privilege of selling your product. These 12 salesmen went out and, for a 50-percent commission, each convinced 12 more (one per month) to do the same.

In a single month this produced 144 salesmen and $3.6 million in revenue: $1.95 million for you, and $1.65 million for your salesmen.

In two months, this produced 1,728 salesmen and an impressive $43.2 million in revenue: $21.9 million for you, and $21.3 million for your salesmen.

Not bad.

But in one year – *just a single year* – if every salesman managed to convince just one additional recruit per month to invest in your company, you would have a sales force of over 8.9 trillion – more than two thousand times the population of the whole world – and revenues of $111.2 trillion: $56 trillion for you, $55.5 trillion for your salesmen.

So okay, some of your salesmen might turn out to be slackers who wouldn't deliver a new investor every month.

But with numbers like these, you could afford a few slackers.

✦

In the fall of 1967, after a short stint with Holiday Magic, Turner borrowed $25,000[*] and founded Koscot Interplanetary, Inc., a cosmetics firm based on the pyramid principle.

He didn't call it that, of course. Pyramid business tactics were actually illegal. But they fell into a grey area that included everything from chain letters (illegal) to franchising (mostly legal). So Turner called his racket "multi-level marketing."

The company sold two products: (a) cosmetics, with a mark-up (for example) of $1.75 per bottle of aftershave; and (b) a variety of "distributorships," costing up to $25,000, which allowed the distributor to bring in an unlimited number of other distributors for a $10,250 commission per newcomer.

In true pyramid fashion, Turner focused primarily on the

---

[*] For consistency, all dollar amounts in this volume have been adjusted to 1990 values.

sale of distributorships. After all, no door-to-door sales company can sell very much without a sales force.

By the fall of 1968, Turner was ready to assess the results.

They weren't, admittedly, quite as amazing as those of copulating houseflies. But in his first year, Turner had convinced 3,640 distributors to join his parade – for a gross cash intake of $80 million.

Not bad, for a start.

As for the actual cosmetics, well, there weren't any yet – Turner hadn't quite got around to that. But nobody seemed to notice or care. The multi-level marketing concept had been bench-tested, and it worked. Now the sky was the limit.

Turner shifted into overdrive. He began to preach the gospel of greed and profits like an evangelist in heat.[*] He quoted Ecclesiastes 10:19 like a mantra: "A feast is made for laughter and wine maketh merry: BUT MONEY ANSWERETH ALL THINGS!" His "Opportunity Meetings," to which each Koscot distributor had to bring a steady stream of new recruits, thumped and roared like Baptist revivals. Hundreds, sometimes thousands, of distributors and their prospects were whipped to a fever pitch by Turner's frenzied incitements to reject the naysayers (Evil), believe in yourself (Good), and sell, sell, sell. They sang and clapped hysterically. They bellowed (to the Sunday-school tune of "This Little Light of Mine, I'm Gonna Let It Shine") *"In my new El Dorado, I'm gonna let it shine; in my new Mark IV, I'm gonna let it shine."* They hummed the money hum. "Mmmmmmmmmmmmmmm . . . MONEY!" And at every opportunity – there were always plenty of opportunities – the whole assembly burst into long,

---

[*] The following and all subsequent quotes are taken from *Dare to Be Great* by Rudy Maxa. See "Sources."

impromptu, fist-waving chants of "GET THAT CHEQUE!! GET THAT CHEQUE!! GET THAT CHEQUE!!

To join Koscot, you had to join THE PROGRAM. THE PROGRAM taught you how to MAKE MONEY. The way you made money was to get new recruits to MAKE THE INVESTMENT. Getting people to MAKE THE INVESTMENT was called HELPING PEOPLE. You helped people get rich by getting them to recruit more people to MAKE THE INVESTMENT. To get people to MAKE THE INVESTMENT you had to get yourself really JACKED UP. The more you talked about MAKING MONEY and MAKING THE INVESTMENT and HELPING PEOPLE, the more JACKED UP you got, and the more JACKED UP you got, the more likely it was that you would GET THAT CHEQUE! GET THAT CHEQUE! GET THAT CHEQUE!

Turner's motivational teams fanned out across the entire United States to help people and get that cheque. By 1969, more than a thousand new recruits were pouring their investments into Koscot's coffers every month. Many had gotten so jacked up, they'd quit their jobs, spent their savings, borrowed the money, or even mortgaged or sold their homes to get on board. Koscot motivators always gave new prospects the distinct impression that annual earnings of $250,000 were routine and almost unavoidable. There were always "financial advisers" available at all motivational meetings to accompany recruits to nearby banks or finance companies, to "help" them make arrangements for their investments, and to shield them from the naysayers who, in Koscot-speak, were called "Martians."

From 1969 to 1971, Koscot averaged more than a 100-per-cent increase in its gross cash intake every year: $120 million, $180 million, $460 million. The number of its distributors kept doubling, too. Within three years there were over 75,000 of them, including Koscot subsidiaries in eight other countries (Canada, Mexico, Venezuela, Australia, England, Italy, Greece, and Germany).

Situated in Orlando, Florida, Koscot's $10-million headquarters was fronted by a huge, richly carpeted circular foyer, finished in expensive wood panelling and arrayed with enormously enlarged photographs of Glenn Turner's childhood as a poor, uneducated sharecropper's son. Turner's office added more telling personal details: sofas upholstered in zebra skin, an enormous, raised, C-shaped desk, backed by a gigantic American flag, two garish paintings (a man and a horse representing Turner's past; a spacecraft representing his future), and a vast white-marble fireplace. The spare tire of a model Rolls-Royce on Turner's desk could be wound up to play "The Impossible Dream."

Turner himself was a more complicated study in contrasts. Outwardly brash and defiant, he loved to flash money and became notorious for stuffing hundred-dollar bills down the cleavages of cheerleaders and beauty contestants. He loved commotion and provocation. As Koscot grew, he took to wearing neon-coloured suits to work and red velvet tuxedoes to more formal occasions. His boots were made of unborn-calf skins, and his hands, shirts, and lapels were always studded with gold and rhinestones. He was particularly anxious about his hair and kept a full-time barber on call in a private barbershop linked to his office by an invisible door.

Despite his pronounced harelip and a nasal voice, women swarmed around him. So did cripples, bankrupts, or anyone else down on his luck. Turner was known as a soft touch – an impulse curiously at odds with his daily business practices. Anyone with a harelip was guaranteed a job at Koscot. Turner also developed a great fondness for a set of twin midgets (both exactly thirty-three inches tall) called John and Greg Rice, from whom he became inseparable. They travelled all over the world with him to Koscot Opportunity Meetings, and often shared the stage with him. "How do you feel, boys?" he'd ask, and their standard answer was, "Like dimes in a bunch of nickels, Mr. Turner."

But while his public manner was expansive and generous, he was also secretive and distrustful. His office walls were lined with sheets of lead, and his desk surface was underlaid with a demagnetizing plate that he could activate with the push of a button. Any reporter who struck Turner as unconvinced or hostile invariably returned to his newspaper office to discover that the tape of the entire interview was unaccountably blank.

Not that Turner's paranoia was entirely unfounded. As his operation expanded, so did the suspicious attentions of both state and federal regulatory agencies. Though consumer-protection laws were in their infancy in many states at this time, it was pretty clear to anyone with even a basic grasp of mathematics that Koscot's pyramid-based business tactics were eventually going to leave an awful lot of people in a financial mess. Actually, this was already beginning to happen. By early 1970, some parts of Pennsylvania, Virginia, and Florida were so saturated with Koscot "distributors" that new recruits were finding themselves forced to travel far afield, often into neighbouring states, to find additional prospects. Protests and complaints began to deluge Koscot's headquarters. The Securities and Exchange Commission in Washington launched an investigation. Lawsuits from disgruntled recruits began to proliferate. State attorneys called on Koscot in growing numbers. By 1971, Koscot's legal department actually outnumbered its motivational staff.

The fact was that Turner's jacked-up sales hype and huge income promises deliberately hid or ignored the fact that most of his new recruits actually *lost* money. When the Pennsylvania

Consumer Protection Bureau finally conducted a formal inquiry into Koscot's activities in that state, they found that 78 per cent of Koscot's recruits *had made no return whatsoever on their $25,000 investment* – and another 13 per cent had made some money but not enough to break even. Of the remaining 9 per cent, most had earned only a modest amount more than their initial investment, and the top distributor for the period examined had earned $98,500 – nowhere near the $250,000 Turner's motivators routinely promised.

But Turner refused to give ground. He had by now defended his crusade to "help the little guy" so often, he undoubtedly believed it himself. For him, multi-level marketing had become an article of faith, a religion, a central feature of being American. The Martians ranged against him were the personifications of everything that kept the little guy down, that kept people from realizing their true potential, that kept much of America "enslaved." Instead of pulling in his horns, he expanded his operations even further, launching the DARE TO BE GREAT Company, a pyramid-based distributor of motivational courses that "sold" its new recruits a cheap briefcaseful of tapes and pamphlets on positive thinking and an accompanying "distributorship" for $25,000.

Predictably, Turner's critics hit the roof. With Koscot, there was at least the appearance of money being paid for products received – each distributor receiving for his "investment" a certain amount of Koscot's cosmetics (which eventually turned up), ostensibly for resale (though everyone knew that, in reality, most of the product just ended up sitting in the distributor's basement). But with DARE TO BE GREAT, what investors received – a handful of tapes – had no resale value at all. Even the pretence of any genuine product-selling had been dropped.

Turner shrugged the critics off. His motivational teams redoubled their efforts. A second, even larger, deluge of money poured into his bank accounts. People began calling him "The Pharaoh of the Pyramids." His pitch, refined and polished by three years' experience, was irresistible.

Everybody, it seemed, wanted to get rich quick at his neighbour's expense.

Turner made sure that his own life-style served as a mobile billboard for DARE TO BE GREAT. His spending, always lavish, became totally extravagant. If he went out to a restaurant and liked the meal, he bought the restaurant. If he liked a shirt, he bought the whole haberdashery. At an Orlando Panthers football game, he became so jacked up about the score, he bought the whole team on the spot. He bought so many expensive cars that he lost track of where he'd parked or stored them. His Lear jets had huge Turner portraits painted on their tails. He built himself an enormous, four-storey castle, complete with moat, drawbridge, turrets, buttresses, and battlements.

There were those who commented darkly that he was going to need them.

There was no doubt that the baying of the legal hounds was getting closer – and louder. Some states had already outlawed DARE or Koscot completely, though Turner sidestepped those blockages by simply busing his recruits to neighbouring states for Opportunity Meetings. The U.S. Securities and Exchange Commission was contemplating hauling Turner into court on security violations. In addition, enough distributors' suits were piling up against Koscot to make a country-wide class-action suit possible. Most ominously, the Postal Service's Mail Fraud Division was getting involved.

The Postal boys were considered absolutely lethal. Their conviction record stood at an astounding 98 per cent.

Turner finally cast about for the best legal muscle that money could buy.

He found his man in F. Lee Bailey.

Bailey, already famous for his brilliant defence of Dr. Sam Sheppard, Captain Ernest Medina, and the perpetrators of the Great Plymouth Mail Robbery, hated the Post Office. He'd just said so at great length in a newly published book, *The Defense Never Rests*. He tended to take anything the Postal boys did personally.

From 1970 to 1972, Bailey defended Turner pugnaciously on a dozen fronts. Taking full advantage of the fuzzier legal aspects of anti-pyramid laws, Bailey fought dozens of state attorneys to a draw. He toned down those of Koscot's business practices that most offended consumer advocates. He brought in business professionals who axed a burgeoning cluster of ancillary companies that weren't making any money: Shucot (shoes), Meatcot (meats), Jewelcot (jewellery), Inscot (insurance). He put out political fires. He brokered legal deals. He meetinged the feds to death.

During his association with Koscot, the company prospered more than it had any right to expect.

But finally, Bailey couldn't afford to defend Turner to the virtual exclusion of all his other responsibilities. In early 1972, he handed the Koscot file to two other colleagues.

From that point on, Turner's fortunes took a nose-dive.

✦

On May 15, 1972, the U.S. Securities and Exchange Commission finally made a move on Turner. It charged him, DARE

TO BE GREAT, and four of his principal officers with twenty-eight counts of violating U.S. securities laws.

Turner's new lawyers chose not to present a defence. They simply tried to discredit the government's witnesses. Turner's executives all took the Fifth Amendment, and Turner, whom the SEC had tried to serve with a subpoena on numerous occasions, kept beyond the reach of the government's sheriffs by spending each trial day aloft in his Lear jet over Portland, Oregon, where the trial was taking place. Overnight, he parked and refuelled his jet across the border in nearby Vancouver, Canada.

He lost the case anyway. His appeal was also overturned.

Now Turner Enterprises was in real trouble. The inspirational multiplying characteristics of multi-level selling that Turner had unleashed were suddenly turning against him. Now it was his lawsuits that were multiplying like copulating houseflies.

Most men would have seen the mathematics on the wall and cashed in their chips.

But not Turner. He'd done too good a selling job on himself.

More and more, he saw himself as a prophet in the wilderness. A maligned prophet. A prophet of Free Enterprise in a wilderness of Government Control.

If he couldn't win in the legal arena, he would win in the arena of public opinion. It had not escaped him that a win in the latter often influenced the results in the former.

Full-page advertisements for Glenn Turner began to appear in America's newspapers.

They showed him photographed from below, larger than life, his fist raised and defiant. The text, arranged in a circle around the photo, read: "LORD GOD, GIVE ME THE STRENGTH AND COURAGE . . . TO CONTINUE THE BUSINESSMAN'S AND INDIVIDUAL'S FIGHT FOR FREE ENTERPRISE. Glenn W. Turner. God Bless You."

Then a billboard. Along the Orlando turnpike, for a monthly rental fee of $25,000, Turner hoisted his likeness onto a billboard so huge, it rivalled those in New York's Times Square. Rising seventy-five feet above a shallow lake, and visible for miles in all directions, his full-colour portrait stood triumphantly against an American flag, its message reading: WELCOME TO ORLANDO, HOME OF THE UNSTOPPABLE GLENN TURNER.

Then his own television show. For $500 per half-hour, Turner bought himself airtime as the Johnny Carson sound-alike on early-morning Florida television. He called his show "Welcome to Our World."

And when that didn't work, he ran for the U.S. Senate.

Whether he was angling for senatorial immunity or just hoping to influence consumer-protection laws is anybody's guess. But there was no question that the job played to Turner's strengths. If anyone could rally a crowd, Turner could. He cranked his salesmanship and charm to the max. He billed himself as the candidate for the little man – the free-enterpriser in a land that was losing its glorious free-enterprise tradition.

Did he really have a chance? Did he have a hope of winning?

It'll be easy, Turner laughed. I'll tell you how to do it. You convince twelve voters of the merits of your crusade. They each convince another dozen, that dozen each convinces a dozen more, and so on, and so on . . . what have you got?

Pyramid politics!

And it seemed to be working. The crowds liked him, and he was clearly in his element. Invitations to rallies, town-hall meetings, public debates, and conventions multiplied.

His PR manager got him invited to a string of international congresses, conferences, festivals. He was asked to give a guest lecture at Harvard.

Turner gloried in all the attention.

"I must be Jesus Christ come again," he marvelled.

In the end, just under fifty thousand voters agreed – creditable, but not enough. The Senate seat went to a corporate lawyer from Miami.

✦

Turner's downfall was not as dramatic as that of Jesus Christ, but it was just as ignominious. By the time all the various state and federal prosecutors had had their day, Turner's billion-dollar empire was a shambles. He finally sold it for a paltry $75,000 to the only buyer who was interested.

But the court cases still kept coming.

Flat broke, Turner finally had to dismiss his last lawyer and represent himself in court. Ironically, he did that better than all his million-dollar lawyers put together. After causing interminable investigations, inquiries, hearings, trials, and hung juries, he was able to negotiate a deal with the government that saw him plead guilty to only as many charges and misdemeanours as would still allow him to take another crack at a Senate seat some time in the future.

In agreeing, the government dropped more than half of its original twenty-eight-count indictment.

Turner's eventual sentence was a $25,000 fine and a short probation, with the fine to be waived if the provisions of the probation were satisfactorily met. The provisions: to report to a probation office three times a year – by mail!

From rise to fall, Turner's business empire lasted only seven years, but in its short life, through the truly inspirational multiplying characteristics of pyramid selling, over a hundred thousand ordinary people lost over a quarter of a billion dollars. Many of them lost all of their savings, and some of them lost their homes.

Glenn Turner, however, was able to keep his political future and his castle.

This was, after all, not a fairy tale.

✦

Update: Glenn Turner ran for the Florida Senate in 1976, but lost again. By 1980 he was once again in the news as the driving force behind a DARE TO BE GREAT copycat company called CHALLENGE TO AMERICA. The company, nominally headed by a former Turner bodyguard, claimed to be sufficiently different in its business methods to avoid Turner's earlier problems, but by the mid-eighties, Turner was once again heavily embroiled with state and federal regulatory agencies. *Plus ça change . . .*

Frozen Assets

Yankee Boondoggle #1

In the fall of 1967, a series of thefts at the state agricultural college in Ames, Iowa, had the police completely stumped.

Somebody was stealing cigarettes out of the college's vending machines. The vending-machine company's agents were reporting smaller and smaller collections, despite steadily increasing sales.

Ordinarily, the explanation for such shortages would be fairly obvious, and so would the evidence: metal slugs in the coin boxes, or physically damaged machines.

Neither applied in this case. None of the machines had been tampered with – and there were no metal slugs.

The vending-machine investigators decided that someone had copied the master key. They changed all the locks on the vending machines. It cost them over a thousand dollars.

But the cigarettes kept vanishing. In fact, the phenomenon began to spread. By December, cigarettes were disappearing from vending machines within a five-mile radius of the college. By February 1968, the epidemic had spread into Ames itself. The police were receiving reports of students selling smokes in bars at cut-rate prices all over the city. Then the selling moved out into the streets.

After four months of investigation, the police were no closer to solving the mystery. Logically, everything pointed to a conspiracy among the vending-machine agents, who serviced and collected the money from these machines. But they had all been interrogated and watched, and none had been implicated. They were, in fact, eager to have this mystery solved, to be cleared of the suspicion and distrust.

The agents reported everything that struck them as unusual. One noted an increased use of portable transistor radios among students. He thought they might house some form of electrical device that could cause the machines to release cigarette packages without coins being deposited. Another had seen several students tossing their coins from hand to hand as if they were hot, making him speculate that heat-expanded coins might become stuck briefly – until they cooled down – in the delivery chute, allowing more than one package to drop. (The company tested this theory on a machine in their service department, with negative results.) Several agents reported seeing small puddles of water under some of the rifled machines, which perplexed them, since the machines contained no plumbing.

But generally, what watchers saw was crowds of ordinary students, dressed in their winter coats and gloves, ambling past the machines in a steady stream, some stopping briefly to buy cigarettes, some buying three or four packages – and, when the machines were checked at one-hour intervals, the cigarettes were invariably gone, the coin boxes had a few paltry coins in them – and sometimes there was a little water on the floor.

It wasn't until the following spring, when all the winter coats came off – and the hats and the scarves and the boots – that investigators noticed a new and curious phenomenon. Though they had shed their winter clothes, many students couldn't seem to give up their gloves. The sun shone brightly, the temperature rose to twenty degrees Celsius, and sandals and shorts replaced jeans and running shoes, but, when they stopped to buy cigarettes at the vending machines, many students promptly reverted to mittens or gloves.

Then the affected areas began to change. As spring progressed, the incidence of rifled cigarette machines abruptly retreated from the town to the college, then to the general area around the Animal Husbandry department. Here, glove-wearing continued unabated, as did the illicit harvest of the cigarette machines. And the size of the water puddles increased.

With this increasingly focused evidence, the Ames police finally swooped in.

What they discovered – rather painfully in the first few instances – was that students had been feeding the machines with slugs *made of super-frozen dry ice.*

The moulds had been provided by an enterprising student, who had used clay-working tools from a first-year pottery class. The "ice" was actually frozen carbon dioxide, unwittingly provided by the college's Animal Husbandry department, whose dry-ice storage facility for bull semen permitted agriculture students to store their slugs at a skin-searing $-78°C$. Such slugs lasted far longer and were a great deal harder than slugs made of ordinary ice, but had to be handled more carefully, too – dry ice "burned" skin like an open flame. Several policemen experienced this dramatically when they triumphantly twisted the evidence out of their suspects' gloved hands.

It could have been the perfect crime, because dry ice doesn't melt like ordinary ice – it evaporates. The evidence was supposed to evaporate without leaving a clue, and it did, but the students had forgotten about condensation. The slugs cooled the coin boxes so quickly that the surrounding warmer air condensed on their outer surfaces, producing the incriminating water.

But the crime turned out to be almost perfect anyway. As soon as the police had caught their first three culprits, word spread like wildfire, and the whole operation evaporated like the dry ice on which it was based. The Animal Husbandry department, which had become more popular than the Students' Union over the winter, abruptly emptied as rapidly as Students' Chapel at three o'clock in the afternoon. Nobody else was ever caught.

The three culprits, meanwhile, really couldn't be charged with anything more than the theft of several packets of cigarettes, a crime hardly worth wasting a magistrate's time. They were each fined twenty-five dollars and put on probation for three months – the entire legal recourse for an investigation that had involved over a dozen investigators, and had cost the Tellmark Vending Company of Iowa over $500,000 in lost revenue and tobacco taxes.

There were reports, in subsequent years, of copycat swindles at a variety of other campuses in the United States, Canada, and England.

The Great Purolator
Paper Caper

Five Jokers in Search of a Savings Account

In 1974, the large, box-like mass of concrete that constituted the Purolator Security Company's Chicago headquarters might well have represented a security aficionado's fondest dream. It bristled with guns and alarms. Armoured-van drivers transported bags of money in and out through a triple-tiered system of double-locked gates, steel doors, and sliding barriers that would have done a maximum-security prison proud. Its counting rooms were encased in tons of steel and bulletproof glass brick. The walls of the massive vault in which its customers' millions were stored had been constructed of two-foot-thick reinforced concrete that was riddled with electronic scanners and ultrasonic alarms. These alarms were connected directly to the alarm board of a nearby Wells Fargo office, which in turn was connected directly to the police.

In short, Purolator's security installations, policies, and procedures had been carefully designed and refined to take into account every security contingency known to forensic science.

Except Ralphie.

Ralphie Marrera was a night watchman at Purolator. The other night guards liked him, because he often volunteered for weekend duty. A night guard's job was pretty boring at the best of times, but weekends were the worst. A guy could go bonkers staring all shift long at the rows of television monitors on which nothing ever happened. For some reason, the boredom never seemed to faze Ralphie. He could be a real bear for that kind of punishment. In fact, he often offered to cover for the other two guards who made up the obligatory threesome at Purolator on weekends, allowing them to go home early or catch a movie at a porn theatre a few blocks away. If you kept your walkie-talkie turned on low, you could still get back in a hurry if anything went wrong.

Fortunately, nothing ever did, unless you counted the false alarms that seemed to proliferate on weekends. They would have really irritated most people, but Ralphie just shrugged them off. These things happen. There was obviously something screwed up in the circuits, but several different electricians still hadn't been able to nail it. The boys down at Wells Fargo got so tired of hoofing it over whenever that damned alarm went off that they took to just phoning Ralphie to check it out. There was never any problem – but somebody was going to have to fix those goddamn circuits sooner or later . . .

✦

A year earlier, not long after he'd landed his job at Purolator, Ralphie had taken to meeting Charlie Marzano regularly for breakfast at Connie's Restaurant on Balsam Street. Like Ralphie, Charlie had grown up in Chicago's Little Italy, and they shared similarly contradictory employment histories. Ralphie, for example, was a lowly paid night guard who also owned a hotel, a gas station, a duplex, and an assortment of other real estate. Charlie was a truck driver who also owned a bunch of real estate and specialized in electronic burglar alarms. (He didn't sell them; he disconnected them.) He was also pretty handy with safe combinations. The two had been implicated, but not charged, in connection with a $2.5-million* jewellery robbery earlier that year. Somehow, this information hadn't come to the attention of Ralphie's superiors.

Charlie introduced Ralphie to his cousin Tony Marzano, another Little Italy alumnus. Tony was a trucker who specialized in bogus credit cards and airline tickets. Unlike Charlie and Ralphie, who'd been married to their first wives for several decades, Tony had been married only briefly and was not in a hurry to repeat the experience. This accounted for his lack of real estate and other financial durables. It also accounted for the considerable daily accumulation of women's messages on his answering machine.

It wasn't long before Charlie invited Pete Gushi to these breakfasts, too. Gushi was the proprietor of a Chicago family discount store who was reputed to be a freelance Mob enforcer on the side. Chicago police had on several occasions suggested to Gushi that his discount store was really just a front for a

---

* For consistency, all dollar amounts in this volume have been adjusted to 1990 values.

large-scale fencing operation. Gushi had been astonished and offended each time.

Gushi introduced his fellow breakfasters to Frankie Bandello (not his real name). Not having grown up in Charlie's and Ralphie's neighbourhood, Bandello was a stockbroker who actually bought and sold stocks. Gushi praised Bandello's remarkable expertise in money laundering, which Bandello was happy to acknowledge. Bandello always loved to acknowledge his own abilities. Actually, Bandello loved everything about himself – especially his hair. At a rough estimate, the men at Connie's Restaurant figured that Bandello must spend about six friggin' hours a day coiffing himself, but what the hell.

After almost ten months of breakfasting, the group decided to invest in the following: a new Econoline van; several Colt 45s and a shotgun; several short-range FM walkie-talkies; rubber gloves and lengths of fuse cord; a variety of electrical gadgets and supplies; a dozen large army-style duffel bags; ten soft vinyl water-bags; some fake ID; and chisels, wrecking bars, and hammers.

Unbeknownst to the others, Charlie – who had evolved as the man in charge – also added the ingredients necessary to make several good-sized bombs.

On Sunday, October 20, 1974, at six o'clock in the evening, a two-vehicle convoy took the Ohio Street exit ramp off the Congress Expressway and headed for the corner of Huron and La Salle, where Purolator was located. The driver of the Econoline van was Charlie Marzano; the sedan was being piloted by Tony Marzano. The two men stopped several blocks from the Purolator building, parked, turned on their walkie-talkies, and waited.

Finally, the sets came alive. "It's okay," Ralphie's voice rasped.[*]

Relief flooded both men's faces. They'd been going through this exercise every Sunday evening for the past three weeks, and every time Ralphie had waved them off. The strain had become a damned nuisance. Now the Econoline pulled out and headed for Purolator's big garage doors on Huron Street. Tony moved his car to the other side of La Salle and parked again. His job was to keep an eye on any outside action until Charlie was ready for him inside. He heard Charlie's voice over the set, talking to Ralphie.

"One to two. I'm ready. Open the door."

A few moments later he heard Charlie's voice again. "I'm here, goddamnit. *Open the fuckin' door!*"

The silence of the next thirty minutes was deafening.

Then, finally, Charlie's voice crackled in Tony's set once again. "Okay. Come on in."

Tony hurried across the street, past several empty Purolator vans, and up to Purolator's overhead doors. He kicked one sharply. It began to hum and rise. Before it was more than three feet up, Tony ducked underneath and it sank down again.

He found himself in a cavernous unlit maintenance garage, with over a dozen Purolator vans parked in rows or raised on jack-stands for repairs. (Purolator did its own servicing to avoid sabotage.) The Econoline stood just inside the overhead door. Charlie beckoned from a nearby stairway, and Tony followed him through a number of short corridors and up several stairs to Purolator's huge vault room. Inside, lit only by Charlie's huge flashlight, stood two massive free-standing vaults, like grim

---

[*] All quotes in this story are paraphrased from *The Big Steal* by Tony Marzano and Painter Powell. See "Sources."

bomb shelters in the murk. The heavy door to the one on the left had already been deactivated and opened. Charlie waved Tony inside. "In here," he said.

And there it was. What Tony saw as his eyes became accustomed to the gloom nearly made him go weak in the knees. All around him, piled almost to the fifteen-foot ceiling, were hundreds of canvas bags and metal footlockers filled with cash. Tons of it. Mountains of it. Millions and millions of dollars. Far more than he'd expected, and – Tony could see this right away – obviously far more than Charlie or Ralphie had planned for, too. The Econoline suddenly seemed absurdly small. There should have been half a dozen guys for this part of the job, and at least another van, maybe three. Maybe four, five. There was enough money here to buy half of Chicago! The same thoughts seemed to be preoccupying Charlie, too, as his flashlight sketched out the outline of this enormous treasure . . .

Finally, Charlie shrugged and handed Tony a set of surgical gloves. "Let's just get started," was all he said.

For the next hour the two packed, hoisted, and dragged like a pair of galley slaves. Charlie cut the seals off the canvas sacks and slung those with large-enough denominations over to Tony, who pulled out the heavy bundles of bills and restashed them in their own duffel bags. After a while, Charlie went to work on some of the footlockers, too. The bundles were at least a foot thick and tightly packed – so tightly, they seemed to weigh as much as an equivalent-sized brick. Tony's hands began to sweat so heavily that the surgical gloves kept slipping off. This was much harder work than driving a truck.

When they had filled four duffel bags, they lurched back down the corridor to the garage. The bags were so heavy, Tony had to drag his along the ground for the last fifty feet, and was barely able to hoist them into the van. Both men hurried back and stuffed the next four bags. This second load seemed even heavier than the first. They shucked their jackets and staggered back in their shirtsleeves.

At some point during all this stuffing and loading, Ralphie's voice crackled through the intercom to report that the second guard (the third had already gone home) had just checked in from the porn theatre via walkie-talkie. Tony wasn't sure whether that was supposed to be a warning to hurry up or just an update, but he allowed himself a brief moment of resentment at Ralphie, who was able to lounge comfortably in front of his bank of monitors, while Tony was busting a gut in this stale-aired vault. Then he dove back into the millions.

When they had packed away as many bundles as their duffel bags could hold, and had stacked everything securely in the van, Charlie deployed the water-bags. He had filled them with gasoline and now planted them strategically around the vault, connecting them like beads on a necklace with a long coil of cotton wick. He attached the end of the wick to a timing device that was set to start a massive fire just after midnight. It would obliterate all traces of the theft. When the police and firemen finally showed up – summoned by the still-intact fire alarms – they would be responding to a fire, not a break and entry.

When everything was set, the two men stood back and took a long last look around the vault.

They seemed to have made barely a dent in all that money. Hundreds of unopened canvas sacks still lay untouched in tall piles around the vault.

It was enough to break a safecracker's heart. And then, on top of that, to burn all that dough. That was perverse is what it was. An offence against St. Dismas, the patron saint of thieves.

"Aw well. We got plenty enough for all of us," Charlie said a little defensively.

Which was exactly the sort of bullshit Charlie would say.

"Come on, let's get out of here," Charlie ordered, and they slammed the vault's door shut.

✦

When the police and the firemen responded to the fire alarm at Purolator Security at 1:12 a.m. on Monday, October 21, they were denied entry by a shotgun-carrying Ralphie, who politely explained that Purolator's security regulations did not permit him to allow more than two persons into the building at any one time. He said he was unaware of any fire, and none of his alarms had gone off to indicate a fire, but he was prepared to open the door to the police chief and the fire chief if they wanted to double-check.

Since the two officials couldn't see any obvious signs of fire, they had no particular objections. Both their crews were exhausted from three previous calls in the area that night, involving large explosions at a massage parlour on North La Salle and at a three-storey rental building on Chestnut Street, plus a false-alarm bomb scare at the Institute of Urban Studies at Loyola University. They told their crews to take a break while they made a quick search of the building.

They found nothing in the basement, and nothing in the large maintenance garage. But they did notice what seemed to be a faint halo of smoke above one of the vaults in the vault room.

Since Ralphie didn't know the combination, the branch manager had to be called.

They waited about half an hour until he arrived. It took him another fifteen minutes to dial in all the codes and twirl the knobs in the right sequences to drop the tumblers. Then he pulled open the door.

A dense black cloud of smoke gushed out of the vault, sending everyone into violent fits of coughing.

"That's arson," the fire chief said.

The inside of the vault turned out to be scorched and smoke-blackened, but otherwise unharmed. Eight plastic bags full of gasoline were found sitting on the floor, linked to two badly burned ones by a cotton wick. A melted timing device lay between them.

It seemed the thief or thieves unknown had forgotten one basic requirement for combustion. A fire needs air. Lots of air. The closed vault's tiny air vent had been designed only to provide enough air for anyone accidentally locked inside.

After a brief, intense blaze, the fire had been completely choked off for lack of oxygen.

The branch manager put in a call to the FBI.

Despite the bungled fire, Chicago's newspapers the next day were immensely impressed. The thieves – obviously very sophisticated experts – had managed to break into one of America's most fiercely defended financial fortresses, defeating a bewildering array of alarms and sensors to get away with over $13 million – the largest single heist of cash in American history. It was bigger than the $10-million Brinks job in Boston in 1950. Bigger than the $11-million Post Office job in Plymouth in 1962. It was even bigger than the famous $12-million Rondout Train Robbery in Lake County in 1924.

Clearly, anyone that proficient would have organized a quick and efficient transfer of the loot to points east or, more likely, to Switzerland or the Bahamas for laundering or stashing. The police, if they were still searching around Chicago, had obviously been left in the dust. The whole operation smacked of an international crime cartel, or a Mob-financed syndicate job.

What really happened was considerably less impressive.

At 9:35 p.m. on the night of the heist, when Charlie and Tony arrived at the home of a friend from whom Tony had "rented" the back-yard garage and basement for the night, they encountered a bit of a problem. The Econoline was too long for the garage.

This became evident when most of the van was inside and only the tail-lights were sticking out. "Come on," Tony hissed, seeing cops in every neighbourhood window and every passing car. "Only a coupla more inches! Move it!"

Charlie complied. The van surged forward. The end wall of the garage buckled, with a crackling of breaking boards and timber. The roof sagged down. They were in.

Counting the money turned out to be a major pain, too. Initial euphoria carried them well into half a million, but after that the work became pretty tiring. They kept getting mixed up in the count. A few drinks helped, and a few more really smoothed things out, but after a certain point they became increasingly dubious about how accurately the count was progressing. By three o'clock the next morning they finally gave up and decided to call it an even $13 million. What was a few hundred thousand one way or the other anyway?

Several quick payoffs followed. Somebody named Frenchy showed up and left with a suitcase containing $600,000. Charlie deposited several suitcases containing Ralphie's share ($5 million) in another garage in another part of town. At a traffic oasis, around 4:30 a.m., Charlie stopped the van and, a few minutes later, a car pulled up really close, a suitcase containing about $300,000 was passed over, and both vehicles sprinted off in opposite directions. By five o'clock both Charlie and Tony were sitting in the parking lot of a Denny's restaurant, waiting to make their final million-dollar drop.

There were only two other cars in the lot, both shiny black Lincoln Continentals. One contained Pete Gushi and his very grumpy wife, who was still dressed in curlers and a faded pink bathrobe. The other contained a very carefully coiffed Frankie Bandello. The two cars should have been parked at opposite ends of the parking lot, but they were sitting right next to each other, with Bandello standing beside Gushi's open window, yakking away. So much for efforts at invisibility.

Everybody waited. And waited. The entire crew sat there like sitting ducks, with almost $7 million in hot greenbacks in the van and a trunkful of loaded guns and walkie-talkies. The minutes ticked by like hours.

By six o'clock, it was clear that the connection wasn't going to show. Charlie decided that Gushi's wife should ditch the million-dollar drop at her place while the rest of them carried on. The plan was to drive straight to Florida with the remaining $6 million, where a boat (arranged by Gushi) was to take them to the Grand Cayman Islands.

Everyone agreed except Gushi's wife, who raised enough stink about being stuck with a trunkful of stolen loot to attract all the attention they had ever tried to avoid. It took Pete fifteen minutes to cool her down. Then Bandello discovered that he'd locked his keys in his car – with the motor running. They had to duck into Denny's, swipe a coat hanger, and break into Bandello's car. Another fifteen minutes. By this time the sun was up and the first breakfasters were arriving at Denny's.

It was a miracle the precinct's cops hadn't yet shown up for their morning doughnuts.

They took to the road, with the money in Tony's Ford, Pete and Bandello taking Bandello's Lincoln as the "crash car" in case of a police roadblock, but Bandello drove so slowly that the two vehicles completely lost touch with each other.

When they finally linked up again, at a roadside restaurant hours later, Pete made some phone calls and came back to report that arrangements for the boat had "fallen through." (Actually, he'd totally forgotten to take care of that little matter.)

Since arranging for the boat had been Pete's primary contribution to the heist, there were a few hard feelings. Some of them were expressed rather tactlessly. Charlie had to firmly restore order.

So it was decided they would *fly* to the Grand Caymans. Since they were by now in Ohio (Tony checked with the waitress), Frankie decided to try an Ohio outfit he'd once flown with: Executive Jet Service. He looked them up in the phone book and discovered they serviced an airstrip several hours' drive away. He made arrangements to hire a small Lear jet for four passengers who he said were flying to the Grand Caymans on a fishing trip. The cost was $14,000.

It took them almost half a day to find the place, what with Pete being a drinker and having to stop at every liquor store between the restaurant and the airstrip, and Tony's fear of flying, which had to be dosed with a lot of Pete's booze. Then, somewhere over North Carolina, the pilot mentioned customs.

Nobody had thought about customs.

At least, not in connection with a rented airplane.

There was no way Charlie wanted the Lear jet's flight crew to see what was in those duffel bags – and they would, if the plane had to be checked through Grand Cayman's customs. The idea with the boat had been to avoid customs altogether.

Another change of plans. "We've got business in Miami," Tony told the pilot. "We'll get off there." The pilot looked puzzled, but just nodded. At Miami airport, Charlie insisted on cramming everybody and everything into a single cab; the cab's trunk was practically dragging along the pavement. Then they couldn't decide where to go. "The Colonnade," Pete said, finally. There were other suggestions, but that was the one the cabbie heard.

They had just arrived at the Colonnade and were dragging their duffel bags across the foyer to the reception desk when Charlie's sudden unease increased to suppressed panic. Everywhere he looked, he recognized faces. And all the faces he didn't recognize looked like cops. It took him only another second or two to realize that they *were* cops. He slammed into reverse and began manhandling his bags back towards the entrance doors. Almost immediately, the others were right on his heels.

Every year, in October or November, Miami plays involuntary host to an annual crooks' convention, at which several thousand of the country's smoothest hustlers and egocentric con men treat themselves to a bimbo-studded blow-out in plain sight of the police. Call it a macho gesture. This year, the month turned out to be October, and the place turned out to be the Colonnade. The Purolator heisters, lugging $6 million in red-hot bills, had walked smack into the biggest gathering of cops and robbers in the United States of America.

Back outside, Charlie hurled his bags into the nearest open cab trunk, helped Tony throw his on top, slammed down the lid, and leaped into the back seat. "Drive," he yelled at the protesting cabbie, who had been trying to argue about the overload. "I don't know where, and I don't give a fuck. Just go!"

Miraculously – unbelievably – they weren't followed.

That night, in a family motel on the outskirts of Miami, Pete and Tony celebrated their astonishing escape with a steady stream of Grand Marniers and cognac chasers in the motel's basement bar. It was pretty shabby, but it looked better and better as the night wore on. Even the awful band that was playing in the bar improved as the liquor bill lengthened. Both men became increasingly talkative, then expansive, and finally – buying repeated rounds for the entire house – downright regal. Exactly when they eventually called it a night, and with whom, is destined to remain forever a mystery, but when they staggered back down to the bar the next afternoon for some ice and some hair of the dog, they discovered they had racked up over $9,000 in booze charges and had even insisted on buying the bar band, for $75,000 cash. The motel manager had a signed contract, written laboriously on a table napkin, that said so. Charlie, for some reason, was furious, and spent the next hour grilling them about what else they might have said or bought.

His mood didn't improve when Frankie brought in the day's *Chicago Tribune*, with a front-page story about the Purolator heist, announcing that Ralphie Marrera had been formally arrested. The news sent Gushi into an alcoholic tailspin, and he ignored Charlie's embargo on phone calls to telephone his wife. He wanted to know whether anybody back in Chicago had connected him with the Purolator heist yet. "Well, if they haven't so far," Charlie yelled when he found out, "they sure as fuck will now, won't they?"

It was clear that some firm decisions had to be made. After

some noisy point and counterpoint, it was decided to send Gushi back home; his unbridled drinking was becoming an increasing liability. Frankie, who still had a clean record and could use the fake ID, would transport the money to the Grand Caymans by commercial airliner. Charlie and Tony would follow on a later flight. Frankie would deposit the money temporarily at the Cayman National Bank and then check into the island's Holiday Inn.

While Frankie got himself ready – and coiffed – the others packed up and checked out. Charlie called a cab for Frankie and stacked the duffel bags on the back seat. While they waited for Frankie to come down, Charlie fretted about this and that and decided the rest of the group would fly out of Fort Lauderdale, rather than Miami. Miami was becoming too hot. Once Frankie was safely on his way, Charlie waved over another cabbie and ordered him to take them to Pompano Airport, several hours farther north. In Fort Lauderdale, just before the airport, they pulled into a motel, had lunch, and then called the airport to make reservations. They discovered that there were no more flights scheduled out of Pompano for either the Caymans, New York, or Chicago that day. Flights were available, however, from Miami.

They had to get back into a cab and drive all the way back to Miami.

As soon as Charlie and Tony arrived at the Holiday Inn in the Grand Caymans, they checked the hotel register for Frankie. He should have been there, registered under the name of Martin. But he wasn't.

The next day they checked the register again. Still no Martin. Just as Charlie was about to initiate some very drastic measures, they saw him. He was sitting cheerfully under one of the palm trees in the lobby. He didn't seem to have any idea how close he'd just come to having a contract put out on his life.

His account of his trip was amusing. The flight had been uneventful. He'd had to get one of the other passengers to help him hoist the heavy duffel bags onto the counter of the Grand Caymans customs office. The customs agent had asked him the usual questions.

"Any alcohol or contraband?"

"No."

"Mind if I have a look?" The agent eyed the bulging bags suspiciously.

Well, what could one say?

"Go ahead."

The agent opened the first bag. No clothes, no personal possessions, no merchandise. He dug towards the bottom, feeling around with his fingers. Nothing. Just solid bundles of U.S. hundred-dollar bills.

He closed the bag.

"Any alcohol or contraband in that bag?"

"No."

"Mind if I have a look?"

"Go ahead."

He groped around that bag, as well. In, around, under; back and forth through all those bundles of bills. There was no alcohol. No drugs. Nothing but half a million dollars in barefaced cash.

"How about those?"

"Same as these. Just money."

The agent closed up the second bag. He didn't bother checking the others. "Okay. Enjoy your stay. Next!"

The three men allowed themselves a burst of raucous,

delighted laughter. The Grand Cayman Islands. Man, oh man.
What a friggin' place.

It took them three more days to divide the money among the
half-dozen banks Frankie had chosen to handle their business.
The going rate for long-term deposits was 12 per cent. Rather
than just blowing all the money and attracting dangerous attention, Charlie had decided to set things up so that each of them
would get a regular paycheque – about $240,000 a year.

Frankie did all the work. Charlie and Tony just signed
papers. Between signing sessions, Charlie windowshopped and
Tony drank. Every night they celebrated the day's business
accomplishments with champagne and expensive wines. The
bar bill alone came to $6,000.

And that wrapped up the score. Bandello and Charlie decided
to stay another day or two, catch a few rays, then move on to
the Bahamas for a few weeks. Until Chicago cooled down.

Tony decided to fly home. He had a toothache.

✦

Around noon on Monday, October 21 – barely fourteen hours
after the Purolator heist had gone down – the FBI had discovered a rather annoying thing. *They had known all about the
Purolator heist – names, dates, places – at least six weeks before it had
even happened.*

In the summer of 1974, a small-time fence named Larry
Callahan had been caught in the act by agents of the Illinois
Legislative Investigating Commission. In return for a suspended
sentence, he'd become an ILIC informer. At the time of the
heist, he'd been working undercover as a clerk (read fence) for
one of Pete Gushi's discount stores.

As early as September 12, Larry had reported to the ILIC that a big score was being planned in the Chicago area. His boss, Pete Gushi, had bragged to him in an expansive moment that he was working on the biggest score of his life, good for five, maybe ten million. There had been a series of breakfast meetings – the names included Charlie Marzano, Frankie Bandello, and others. There was talk of hiring a boat in Miami. There was even a scheduled date: September 29, 1974.

All this was passed on to the Illinois Bureau of Investigation, and to the FBI as well. Everybody agreed that this looked like a live one. The IBI climbed into the driver's seat and started the engine. All three organizations contributed agents, investigators, and pen-pushers. The operation gathered momentum.

Everybody on Callahan's list was put under surveillance – and that started paying dividends almost immediately. Within minutes of the purchase of the Econoline van, the IBI knew about it. It knew the registration and the licence number. Less than a day after Charlie received the fake ID he'd ordered, the agency had a complete record of it. It soon had a list of the names and backgrounds of everybody with whom Charlie Marzano or Pete Gushi had met from mid-September on, day or night. As soon as Tony Marzano was brought into the picture, they knew about that, too.

The only person they didn't know about – for reasons that have never made sense to anyone – was Ralphie Marrera.

As the countdown to September 29 approached, the law authorities knew virtually everybody and everything connected with Marzano's planned score – *except his target*. This information proved maddeningly elusive. And it didn't help when September 29 came and went without incident. The word from Callahan was that the van hadn't been ready. A week later it was, but still nothing happened. Nothing happened from October 7 to October 14, either.

At this point, the tri-level operation fell apart. None of the three government agencies had the resources to chase after a will-o'-the-wisp. Maybe a score had been planned, maybe it hadn't; whatever the case, it had obviously disintegrated. That happened all the time. Con men and thieves were notoriously unstable. Ninety per cent of what they planned never got off the ground. So the operation was scrapped, the reports were filed away, and each agency went about its business.

One week later, the biggest heist in the history of the United States caught them all with their pants down.

In criminal investigations involving seasoned crooks, any lawman worth his salt looks immediately for the weakest link and works from there.

There isn't much hope otherwise. Crime movies and police propaganda to the contrary, most cases are eventually cracked by the use of informers or stool pigeons. All the investigative powers in the world don't add up to much on their own. The Purolator heist was virtual textbook proof of that maxim.

Within a few days of the crime, the police had reconstructed the whole story. They had pieced it together in amazing detail. They knew exactly who had done what, when, how, where, and with whom. But they couldn't have touched a single one of the perpetrators without a witness on the stand who was prepared to point the accusing finger.

On the face of it, this wasn't likely. There had been no witnesses to the robbery. There was no stolen money in hand, and what evidence there was was completely circumstantial. Ralphie Marrera remained impregnable to all efforts at interrogation. His cohorts had been able to cross seven state lines and a dozen jurisdictions, leaving a trail so wide and messy that a child should have been able to find or follow them, but the FBI had missed every opportunity to do so.

So a weak link had to be found – and it was. The astounding thing was *who*. It was FBI bank-robbery-investigation co-ordinator Ramon Stratton who used his gut instinct to decide on Pete Gushi as his primary target. Pete Gushi, Stratton had discovered, had once tried to commit suicide during a short stint in Leavenworth.

To most people, it still seemed an awfully long shot. Gushi was a seasoned crook, with high-level Mob connections and an intimate knowledge of what invariably happened to stoolies. He had probably delivered the Mob's justice to a few such "weak links" himself. Besides, he wasn't facing a murder rap; this was just a paper crime, and, though the amount was large, it had belonged primarily to banks. You couldn't always count on juries to get enormously sentimental about bank losses.

So, rather than a frontal attack, Stratton worked his way in from the side. He pulled together all of Larry Callahan's damaging undercover evidence and spread it out for Gushi's edification. The two cases weren't directly connected, but they could be made to be. When Gushi seemed less than convinced, Stratton hit him with a whole truckload of charges based on Callahan's evidence and testimony about the goings-on at Gushi's discount store. After several days in jail, Gushi was released on $30,000 bail, but he made it only as far as the court-house parking lot. Stratton's boys promptly picked him up again, pending charges related to the Purolator case – and this time he wasn't granted bail. The net around him tightened.

It's not clear exactly which straw broke Gushi's back – certain critical conversations between him and Stratton were kept off the record – but the prospect of twenty to thirty years behind bars obviously had its effect. A week later Gushi agreed to turn state's evidence, in return for a minimal sentence, a new identity under the Witness Protection Program, and no unduly probing questions about what his wife had done with the million dollars.

That cracked the case for Stratton. The domino effect had begun.

Ralphie Marrera was indicted on October 28. Tony Marzano was arrested and charged on October 30. He pleaded not guilty. One day later, Charlie Marzano and Frankie Bandello were caught trying to fly from the Grand Caymans to Costa Rica. They were immediately extradited to the United States to face charges relating to the Purolator robbery. They pleaded not guilty, too.

By November 1 – less than two weeks after what the media had characterized as the slickest, most successful multi-million-dollar theft on record – every one of the thieves was in jail.

The FBI case went from strength to strength. On November 21, a second, unidentified informer suggested the FBI search a house on the outskirts of Chicago that was owned by Ralph Marrera. When the police examined the basement, they found bags containing $2 million buried under a new slab of concrete. A week later Ralphie tried to hang himself in Winnebago County Jail, and, shortly after that, he came down with a mysterious illness that plunged him into a coma. His stomach was pumped and he was revived, but he remained, according to court records, in a "dazed condition."

Next, the FBI was able to show that the Marrera money was marked – it had been marked by a local race-track, which had then transferred it into Purolator's custody on the day before the robbery. That proved beyond a doubt that Marrera's money had been stolen.

Finally, one of Tony Marzano's fingerprints was found on one of the stolen bills.

Tony Marzano changed his plea to guilty.

By any sort of logic, that should have clinched the case for the FBI.

But as anyone who works in the legal system knows, it ain't over till the Fat Lady sings. After a week-long trial during April 1975, Ralph Marrera was found unfit to stand trial. Frankie Bandello was found not guilty when the evidence proved unconvincing. Pete Gushi got a mere fourteen months (just long enough for the FBI to set him up with a new identity and a new address), and Tony Marzano got seven years, later reduced to five, of which he served only twenty-eight months. In fact, from the FBI's point of view only Charlie Marzano received a sentence remotely commensurate with his crime: twenty years – but his sentence, too, was later reduced, to fifteen.

Which left the little matter of the $6 million still earning interest in the Grand Caymans. But if Frankie, Charlie, and Tony had any thoughts of keeping that nest egg for a rainy day, the rain stopped falling right after their trial. In October 1975 the Attorney General of the Grand Cayman Islands, in an unprecedented move, quietly prevailed on the six banks in question to return the money to Lloyd's of London (Purolator's insurers) and they did – with approximately $1.5 million in interest.

And that's when the Fat Lady finally started yodelling.

For Export Only

Shamrock Shenanigans #2

The greatest economic problem that faced the Republic of Ireland during the 1960s and 1970s was its poor export performance. As a result, by 1975, Eire was in desperate need of foreign currency.

To encourage an exports revival, Eire's government announced an incentive program that would pay Irish exporters a 4-per-cent bonus for each £1,000 (Irish) worth of exports. The payments would be made upon presentation of all bills of lading duly stamped and initialled by an Eire customs office.

The program proved remarkably successful. Exports of woollens and whiskey for 1976 recorded creditable increases, as did those of Irish leather products. But the largest improvements by far were recorded for cattle exports. In fact, the program seemed to have encouraged the creation of dozens of new beef-cattle breeding operations, mostly small but remarkably vigorous, whose soaring export sales were lifting industry-wide averages to their highest level since 1942.

One such operation was Flaherty Farms, owned and operated by one Seamus Flaherty. His remarkable ability to find buyers for his beef cattle in neighbouring Northern Ireland (from whence they were presumably shipped to Britain) was a showpiece of efficiency and enterprise. During the first six months of 1976 alone, Flaherty Farms had exported 630 animals, and was well on its way to exceeding that performance in its second half-year.

Curiously, one of the more interesting statistics these cattle sales demonstrated was a hitherto unrecognized, remarkable demand in Northern Ireland for beef on the hoof – something Eire's agricultural officials hadn't previously realized. A bit embarrassing, really, such a strong market going virtually unnoticed on your own doorstep, but if an export incentive program could flush such profitable facts out of the woodwork, so much the better. The purpose was being doubly achieved.

By early December 1976, the figures for cattle exports were still growing. Everyone at the Irish Department of Agriculture preened and congratulated themselves. There were promotions, commendations. The program was working beyond expectation.

And then, on December 22, 1976, a curious incident occurred at the border-patrol station between Eire and Northern Ireland at the village of Clones.

When Seamus Flaherty, crossing the border with ten cows for export, opened the back of his truck for the customs officer, they found themselves confronted with nine cows' heads and one cow's rump. The way the cows were wedged in, there was clearly no room for any of them to turn around. Yet all of them, Flaherty said, had been loaded in rump first. How had one cow managed this impossible feat?

Flaherty and the customs officer chatted idly about this while the officer checked the ear-tags and signed and stamped Flaherty's waybill. They came to no conclusion, and it was only small talk anyway. But because the officer had to climb over the backs of the other nine cows to read the tenth cow's ear-tag, he particularly noticed the hourglass-shaped blaze on the tenth cow's forehead. He remembered it, because its two halves were so unusually balanced and well-proportioned.

And that was all. A brief, curious incident of no particular significance, and certainly nothing the officer would have considered worthy of note in his customs log. When he handed Flaherty the completed waybill, the cattle farmer thanked him cheerfully and wished him a good weekend. Then his truck disappeared down the Monaghan Road.

A subsequent incident that *did* strike the customs officer as noteworthy occurred almost two weeks later, when Flaherty showed up at the same border crossing with another ten cows for export.

This time, when Flaherty opened the rear door for inspection, all his cows were lined up the same way. No rumps this time. Ten bovine faces.

And one of the faces was imprinted with an hourglass-shaped blaze.

The officer didn't mention this to Flaherty, but he did memorize the number on this cow's ear-tag. When Flaherty drove off, he entered the number in his customs log.

When Flaherty showed up again three weeks later, and once

again one of his cows sported an hourglass-shaped blaze, the officer checked its tag against his log notation.

The result was disappointing. The number was totally different.

The officer thought about this for a while, and again didn't mention it to Flaherty. But while the cattle breeder was relieving himself at the station's urinal, the officer used a felt-tip pen to mark the back of the cow's right ear with a fat black dot.

He found it again when Flaherty came through with another ten cows three weeks later. It was still on the back of the right ear of the cow with the hourglass-shaped blaze.

In the uproar that followed, at least part of Flaherty's *modus operandi* was duly unravelled.

Flaherty had not, during 1976, exported a total of 1,340 cows to Northern Ireland as departmental records proudly showed.

He had exported the same ten cows 134 times.

How he'd managed this was simple enough. Flaherty had grown up in Castleblayney, not far from the Eire–Northern Ireland border. He'd become familiar with every border crossing for miles around, and with many of its "unofficial" crossings, too. There were dozens of trails and dirt-track lanes that crisscrossed the border without showing up on official maps.

On a typical day he would drive to an official border crossing from the Eire side, have his cows inspected and his waybill signed, then drive a few miles farther into Northern Ireland before veering off onto a side road that led to one of those unofficial crossings. Re-entering Eire, he would stop just long enough to change his cows' ear-tags – matching them up with a new set of waybills – then drive to another official crossing and register the cows all over again.

On a good day he could repeat that performance as many as six times before a late supper.

Flaherty, it turned out, wasn't now and hadn't ever been a cattle breeder. He was an out-of-work auto mechanic whose entire experience with beef cattle had been limited to loading and unloading them. He didn't own a farm. All he owned was a truck. The cows had lived on that truck more or less permanently for the past year, with brief interruptions for cleaning.

That was all that could be said with any certainty about Seamus Flaherty's operations, because he had been caught only as the proprietor of Flaherty's Farms. Departmental authorities quickly realized that his 134 crossings under that name were probably only the tip of the iceberg; at six per day, he could have made a thousand crossings a year. And indeed, a policeman's discovery of a stash of different licence plates, and cryptic entries in an impounded notebook, indicated that Flaherty may well have been operating as many as half a dozen different paper farms, regularly alternating among names and businesses to avoid undue cross-referencing at border crossings. His ten cows probably represented thousands of exported cows that had pushed the department's 1976 performance figures to their astronomical heights.

For his Flaherty Farms exports, Flaherty had received some £35,000 (Irish) in government bonuses – about $150,000.[*] A Dublin magistrate made him pay that back, and also spend a year and a half in jail.

---

[*] For consistency, all dollar amounts in this volume have been adjusted to 1990 values.

But if departmental suspicions about the range of his operations were correct, this cattle-exporting auto mechanic may have received as much as seven times that amount – over a million dollars.

Proving once again the undeniable efficacy of the modern admonition: "Reduce, Reuse, Recycle."

Brand-Name Crime

———◆·◆———

The High-Quality Exploits of Albert Spaggiari

From as early as he'd been able to afford it, Albert Spaggiari had always opted for top quality. His clothes were made on the Champs Elysées, his shoes by Bonaparte. He drove a superbly maintained Land Rover with all the options.

It wasn't that Spaggiari liked flash or splash. Actually, Spaggiari despised opulence for its own sake. What Spaggiari liked – what he'd insisted on all his life – was comfort and reliability.

As a competitive youngster, born into a poor Italian family in Narbonne, France, in 1951, he'd never forgotten the potential game-winning goal he'd missed when his soccer boot had disintegrated during an overtime penalty kick. He'd suspended that boot from the ceiling of his basement room, and for years it hung there as a reminder. In the late 1960s, serving with the

French army in Indo-China, Spaggiari was court-martialled twice for replacing his army-issue Chernier ITU-44 rifle, which had a tendency to jam when hot, with an extremely expensive AKA-673 Borkalov repeater, which didn't. "It's my life you're risking by issuing me that piece of junk," he pointed out to the military judge, who obviously didn't care. "And besides, I paid for it myself."

Only the last statement was untrue. The one drawback to an obsession with quality was that it usually cost more than Spaggiari could afford. He had discovered this quite early in his life. As a ten-year-old, in 1961, he'd tried to solve the problem by petitioning a famous Marseilles Mafiosi, about whom he'd read in the newspaper, asking to join his gang. Gangsters, Spaggiari had noticed, rarely had trouble paying for quality. This gangster, however, hadn't written back.

Rebuffed by the Mafia, Spaggiari knocked on the door of the next underworld over. The army, which immediately sent him to serve in Indo-China, proved an ideal place to pursue his uncompromising financial ambitions. While training to become a paratrooper and earning three high-level medals for bravery, Spaggiari used his off-duty hours to form a paramilitary brotherhood that knocked over so many Vietnamese nightclubs and smuggled in such quantities of superior Czechoslovakian weaponry that, when he was dishonourably discharged from the army four years later, he was rolling in money.

Now footloose and fancy-free, Spaggiari hung about the city of Nice for several years, running arms for right-wing political organizations and acquiring a taste for 1961 Bordeaux and Dom Miguel cigars. He was considering his longer-term options. All in all, they looked pretty good. Since the collapse of Marseilles as the capital of Continental crime (following the uproar over the Marseilles-based "French Connection"), every big-time bank robber, drug-lord, and con man in France seemed to be gravitating to Nice. The money that accompanied them was swelling the city's coffers. The technical support that followed them was making it possible to plan much more reliably. You could draw on more and more high-quality expertise for an ever-widening range of criminal enterprises.

But perhaps Nice's biggest drawing card in the 1970s was the downtown branch of its Société Générale, on the corner of the rue de l'Hôtel des Postes and the rue Deloye. This bank was famous all over Europe for the impregnability of its safety-deposit vault. Its reinforced concrete walls were said to be six feet thick. Massive, electrically controlled locks secured its armour-plated double doors. A variety of sophisticated electronic systems were said to monitor it day and night. All this had soon become the bank's greatest selling feature: for complete peace of mind, store your valuables at the Société Générale. Many rich and famous people from all over France had taken this advice.

France's crooks, it appeared, were no less interested in this kind of security. Many of them – as Spaggiari discovered, meeting them in Nice's bars and cafés – also stockpiled their loot in the Société Générale. The Société's vault reportedly contained four thousand oversized deposit drawers. Discretion was absolute. It was like having the protection of a Swiss banking system in your own back yard.

The more Spaggiari heard about these deposit drawers, the more he became convinced he should be renting one, too.

In the fall of 1975, Spaggiari conducted his first piece of business with the Société Générale. He signed up for drawer no. 3164 under the name of Yves Montepellier.

The drawer was indeed oversized. There was no doubt that it could accommodate an impressive collection of valuables. But Spaggiari didn't deposit any valuables. He put in an alarm clock set to ring at 11:30 p.m. Three days later he put in a battery-operated timed radio, set to broadcast loudly at 3:30 a.m. Then he deposited a tiny handmade stick of dynamite, wired to a minuscule detonator controlled by a travel-sized alarm clock. When he returned the following week, his drawer was black and scorched from the mini-explosion, but there had been no reaction from the vault's guards or banking personnel.

Once again Spaggiari had to face up to the fact that the world's dedication to quality and reliability was not always as advertised.

So the vault's entire claim to impregnability seemed to lie in its six-foot-thick concrete walls – assuming, of course, they really were six feet thick. Spaggiari paid an employee of the Nice City Works and Sewer Department 500 francs under the table for a map of the city's underbelly. The map proved inconclusive about the vault's wall thickness, but showed a storm sewer passing a mere twenty-six feet to the east of it, heading towards the Paillon River, which flowed beneath the city through an aqueduct. It also showed a handy entrance into that sewer via a manhole in front of the Islam Café, about half a mile from the bank.

It did not escape Spaggiari's notice that a good deal of comfort and reliability might be acquired by putting this information to imaginative use. But the job would require an unprecedented amount of manpower and equipment.

Spaggiari spent the next six months assembling both. When he was ready to begin, on the night of Wednesday, April 7, 1976, he went to work with a crew of sixteen (including four drilling specialists, four welders, an electronics technician, a mechanic, an electrician, a cook, and a jeweller), a fleet of three trucks (including a panel van painted with the colours and logo of the Nice Sewer Department), two cars, a trailer, a splendid set of Hammerstone electric masonry drills, two Truffoni electric jackhammers, a deluxe ten-kilowatt Honda generator and floodlights, a mineshaft-quality Persiflex ventilating fan and dust-filter, four Fournier blowtorches and two oxygen lances, two Siemens arc-welders, and a whopping forty tanks of liquid oxygen.

As an afterthought, he added a set of Rigoletto lawn chairs, a mineral-water dispenser, a case of Château Bourgognie 1956, and a box of good cheeses and pastries from the Boulangerie Louis XIV on the rue de l'Hôtel des Postes.

The work proved hard, wet, bitterly cold, and indescribably filthy. The sewer walls were covered from top to bottom with a six-inch coating of rotting slime, and, as the men stumbled back and forth in the darkness, hauling dirt and rocks from the excavation site to a fast-flowing culvert three hundred yards away, discharges from smaller pipes above their heads drenched them repeatedly with raw sewage and industrial wastes. Thousands of rats scurried and swam all around them, and a bitterly cold wind knifed and moaned through the tunnels day and night.

It was definitely not your average bank job, and the men were often taxed to their limits. But the equipment worked more reliably than any of them had experienced before, and their meals arrived in take-out boxes from the city's most expensive restaurants. Coffee breaks included servings of the finest pastries and pastilles Nice's bakeries could supply, and, when the men struggled back to the surface after seven-hour shifts on weeknights and rotating twelve-hour shifts on weekends, hot baths awaited them in a huge villa that Spaggiari had rented on the city's outskirts.

Actually, it was often more than a hot bath that awaited them. Spaggiari had even added a prostitute to his crew, who, for an equal share of the expected loot, kept house and gave the men something to look forward to while they sweated and strained underground.

So the work progressed well, all things considered. During their first weekend of continuous digging, his men achieved five feet of tunnel. By the following weekend it had lengthened to eight. Then they hit a gigantic rock, so large it was impossible to dig around, and they had no alternative but to drill straight through. That took them three whole weeks. Six days later a gas main not shown on Spaggiari's map brought progress to a standstill once again, but the men showed remarkable ingenuity in rerouting the pipe without interrupting the gas flow, and no one above was the wiser. Spaggiari deployed regular patrols with radios along the street above the worksite to monitor for any sights or sounds of trouble, but since the tunnelling was going on more than eight feet below, the noise at this point was barely audible.

That changed dramatically once the jackhammering reached the bank's foundations. As the massive chisels bit into the concrete, all the building's vents and gratings began to vibrate. The whole building shook and its windows rattled. Horrified, Spaggiari's street patrol radioed frantically for the diggers to stop. Had the bank actually kept an after-hours guard on duty full-time and on weekends, as its depositors no doubt assumed, or had the vault's walls been fitted with the seismic alarms that were already standard among the bank's competitors, the red lights would have lit up like Christmas decorations at the police headquarters only half a mile down the street. But the Société

Générale had negotiated a less-expensive agreement with a night guard who simply looked in on the bank once or twice a night. Occasionally a passing policeman looked in through the windows as well, but since both inspections were visible from the street, Spaggiari's street patrol was always able to radio warnings in advance. As a result, the weekend tunnelling, now performed entirely with electric drills and picks, could continue virtually around the clock.

By the time Spaggiari's diggers had penetrated to the vault's back wall – which, as Spaggiari had suspected, wasn't six feet thick – they had been on the job for over three months. Fortunately, their aim had been right on target. Everyone worked more carefully now, digging by hand with ice picks and augers, not wanting any breaks or cracks to appear on the vault's inner wall until they had a full weekend to break through and loot the boxes. Spaggiari even brought in lengths of carpeting for the tunnel's floor, to muffle accidental sounds.

Finally, when they were fairly sure they were within a foot or so of the inside, they stopped, cleared away all remaining rubble, and waited for the next weekend.

Three hours after closing time on Friday, July 16, 1976, their churning masonry drill suddenly whined aloud and began to free-wheel. Light appeared around the bit's spinning shaft. The driller quickly widened the hole with a chisel. Everyone stopped and waited breathlessly. But no alarms went off and no sirens sounded. The driller now enlarged the hole enough to squeeze inside. Spaggiari handed through some electronic sensing equipment and climbed in himself. Before anyone else followed, he checked the entire vault for any other form of alarm. There was none. The men began to pass in the cutting and welding equipment.

Within half an hour the vault was transformed into a surreal amalgam of welding shop, bazaar, cafeteria, art gallery, and flophouse. In one corner, the cook set up two butane camp-stoves and prepared to feed sixteen men through an entire weekend. In another, forty tanks of oxygen were set up to feed four cutting torches on a round-the-clock schedule. Half a dozen sleeping bags lay piled against the vault's doors, and a table was set up for the jeweller, to evaluate the jewellery on the spot. As the welders began to attack the first safety-deposit boxes, Spaggiari paced the vault impatiently, puffing on his habitual Dom Miguel cigar.

The first box contained little more than papers: passports, certificates, personal documents.

The second box contained a huge collection of porno-graphic photographs.

But what they found in the third, fourth, and fifth drawers – and then on average three times out of five – exceeded their wildest dreams.

The drawers were bursting with cash, bullion, jewellery, art, and securities. The contents of the third, fourth, and fifth drawers alone spilled a veritable king's ransom into the dust and rubble on the vault floor. For a few moments, until Spaggiari re-established order, the men flung bills and securities into the air like confetti. The vault began to look like the aftermath of a Mediterranean wedding. When sanity returned, Spaggiari ordered that the looting was to proceed in a more systematic fashion.

The four welders set to work slicing away the locks and hinges with cutting torches. Four others smashed the drawers open with hammers and crowbars. Spaggiari and a partner made quick decisions about what to take and what to leave. Any jewellery was given to the jeweller for a yes or a no. Five men packed the loot into canvas army bags and dragged them out to the sewer. The cook prepared sausages and eggs, with béarnaise sauce.

They all worked briskly and quietly now. Once in a while someone exclaimed over a particularly large or expensive piece of jewellery or an unusually large bundle of high-denomination bills, but Spaggiari wanted to keep an ear tuned to the bank's front door, in case the police decided to make an exception and take a look inside. Fortunately they didn't. The men were able to continue without interruption for the next twelve hours, and even then only half the crew flopped down on sleeping bags for a brief nap while the other half laboured on.

By now the vault was like a sauna from all the flame and smoke and cooking. Its ventilation system was severely over-loaded. All the men had stripped down to their underwear and were pouring with sweat. The fumes from a broken bottle of rare perfume added a sickening overlay to the acrid stench. Heaps of discarded jewellery, non-negotiable securities and – to everyone's surprise – large amounts of spoiled and rancid food that had been stashed in a number of drawers, grew steadily higher around the five drawer-smashers. The steamy scene was made all the more lurid by the hundreds of large pornographic photographs lying scattered all over the floor and against the vault's walls.

At ten o'clock on Sunday morning an alarm call from the street patrol warned of the approach of the bank guard. Everyone switched off their torches and dropped their tools. Most of the men found a free patch of floor for another quick catnap. They fell asleep instantly. The jeweller, who'd been on deck nonstop for thirty-six hours, slumped forward onto his table and passed out. Spaggiari swallowed a handful of benzedrine, handed things over to a partner, and squeezed out into the tunnel. He intended to climb up to the street, get cleaned up, make himself noticeable at a nearby restaurant, buy a round at a local café – whatever would provide him with a workable alibi in case of future trouble.

That's when he noticed something that immediately triggered alarm bells in his brain.

The level of water was higher than usual in the storm sewer.

Spaggiari got on the radio to the street patrol. He asked what the weather was doing up there.

The man topside said it was raining.

It wasn't just raining. It was pouring. As soon as Spaggiari climbed out through the manhole at the Islam Café, his heart sank. In the eastern sky, all he could see was grey. No thin pencil-line of white just above the horizon. No mitigating chiaroscuro of mottled cloud-outlines suggesting less than a full-scale rainstorm. Nothing but solid, unrelieved grey.

Temporarily abandoning the idea of the alibi, he hastened back into the sewer. By now his men had also noticed the rapidly rising water, which had already reduced the headroom of parts of the route to the Islam Café to less than four feet. At this rate, that exit would be unusable in about two hours. There was a larger connection, at a point where Nice's sewers emptied into the enormous underground aqueduct of the Paillon River, which plunged beneath the city through a set of high archways beneath the Palais des Expositions. But that was over a mile and a half upstream.

There were really only two options: continue looting the vault for another ninety minutes or so, then escape through the Islam Café entrance at the last possible minute. Or – a far riskier proposal – continue looting until the water rose right up to the level of the sewer's walkways (less than five feet below the ceiling), then pile all the loot into several inflatable zodiacs and hand-haul them through a mile and a half of seething storm sewer to the archways beneath the Palais des Expositions.

They chose the second option.

The work inside the vault now sped up to a frantic pace. During the preceding two days they'd averaged about half a dozen drawers an hour. Now they doubled that number. The vault was soon three feet deep in discarded securities and documents. Everyone slipped and skidded on hundreds of parchments, passports, and velvet or silk casings. Once a still-glowing piece of drawer hinge ignited a stray five-hundred-franc note and only the cook's quick reaction with a jug of mineral water averted a major disaster. Everyone tried not to notice the increasingly alarmed looks on the faces of the men who were hauling the bags out to the sewer.

Shortly after midnight on Sunday, one of the packers called Spaggiari aside. He asked him to come out and see for himself.

What Spaggiari saw was enough to make his blood run cold. What had been merely a dark and quietly churning creek over four feet below their walkway at 8:45 earlier that evening was now a wildly foaming torrent, crashing past at tremendous speed. It had risen to just a few inches below the walkway, and the racket was terrifying. Their escape, if the water kept rising at this rate, would be cut off within the hour.

There was no time to lose. Spaggiari ordered two men to inflate the zodiacs, while he crawled back into the bank and called a halt to the operation there. Each man finished up what he was doing and shut down his equipment. The last piles of treasure were thrown pell-mell into bags and sacks and flung into the tunnel. One after another, the men disappeared into the same hole. Less than ten minutes later, Spaggiari was the only man left in the vault.

He looked around, grimacing. The sight was no less moving than the one outside – if for somewhat different reasons. Even working at breakneck speed, they'd been able to empty only about 10 per cent of the vault's drawers. What a monumental waste! To have gotten their hands this firmly on one of the biggest accumulations of treasure in all of France, only to have to let go again. Spaggiari picked up a German 1,000-Deutschmark banknote he'd kicked up with his boot, and then dropped it again, sighing. There was nothing to be done.

Except perhaps to make pursuit just a little more difficult. Spaggiari ignited the arc-welder and carefully spot-welded the vault's massive front door shut from the inside. That would keep them busy for a few extra hours on Monday morning.

Back outside, the zodiacs were inflated and packed, but they weren't big enough to carry all the loot. Everyone shouldered the remaining knapsacks and army bags. The rest of the equipment had to be abandoned. The din of the roaring water was now so loud, the only way to communicate was by pantomime. Everyone was worried, and some men were clearly terrified. The water had already risen several inches over the walkways and was surging over everyone's boots. It had become impossible to tell any more exactly where the walkway's left-hand edge fell away into deep water.

They set off, carefully feeling their way. Every few minutes someone's left foot slipped off the walkway, bringing him lunging and flailing to his knees. Flashlight beams seemed almost useless against the bellowing blackness. The men towing the zodiacs couldn't maintain headway against the current and had to be doubled, then tripled up. Before the struggling column had even reached the Paillon River, two of the men had become so exhausted they refused to go on and had to be forced with threats and blows. In a number of smaller connecting sewers without walkways, ropes had to be strung from one end to the other to help the men carrying the heaviest loads to maintain footing and headway. The jeweller, a very short man, lost both, and was swept back down into the sewer's throat, his screams inaudible over the water's thunder. Luckily he was flung against a low-hanging waterpipe and the flashlight hanging from his neck enabled the men to find him. He was unconscious, possibly drowned. Somebody flung him over his shoulder and dragged him the rest of the way like a sack of potatoes.

The first men of the column reached the safety of the Paillon River's subterranean entranceway at 3:20 that morning. The rest appeared in twos and threes over the next hour and a half, staggering along almost comatose, stupefied with exhaustion. The jeweller, looking indistinguishable from the pile of soaked and muddy army bags onto which he'd been dumped, proved to be still breathing. At that moment, nobody cared much one way or the other. Spaggiari, swallowing another fistful of benzedrine, lurched off to bring the Land Rover down a nearby access road.

The final stragglers found the entire crew huddled heedlessly around its spectacular booty, fast asleep. When Spaggiari drove up an hour later, catching them all in the blaze of his headlights, nobody even stirred. He had to pour water over their heads and bellow into their ears to get them moving.

✦

By the time the police managed to get into the Société's vault, late Monday afternoon, Spaggiari's trail had cooled considerably.

It cooled even further when, in view of the expert tunnelling and the first-class drilling equipment, the police at first concluded their quarry was an engineer or an ex-miner. Their futile stabs in that direction wasted three additional months. By that time, most of Spaggiari's confederates had cashed in their loot and flown the coop. But Spaggiari liked Nice, and had decided to stick around.

Maybe he shouldn't have. The police, under tremendous pressure from the bank and Nice's municipal authorities, used every bit of influence they had on Nice's underworld, and finally somebody cracked. In the end it was Spaggiari's reputation for thoroughness and his fondness for Dom Miguel cigars that did him in. Having found plenty of evidence of both in the vault, not to mention the Rigoletto lawn chairs and several bottles of Hospices de Beaune 1943 – the police arrested Spaggiari on June 25, 1977, almost a year after the break-in, charging him and confederates unknown with the theft of $100 million[*] worth of gold, banknotes, and other valuables. It constituted, to that date, the largest single bank heist in recorded history.

The charge launched Spaggiari well and truly on a career as a French folk hero. Thoroughness and an appreciation of quality had always been considered by the French to be among their most prominent virtues – along with dash, panache, and a goodly shot of derring-do. Spaggiari clearly exemplified all five. And it did him no harm when the newspapers reported, after three months of police interrogations and threats, that Spaggiari had disdained to even consider plea-bargaining.

---

[*] For consistency, all dollar amounts in this volume have been adjusted for 1990 values.

Still, Spaggiari was now on a course leading straight to a twenty-year prison term, and there was very little quality and comfort in that. His lawyer was doing his best, but the court had clearly made up its mind. The rat had been caught, and now the rat would pay.

So Spaggiari made up his own mind, too.

Every Thursday, Spaggiari was taken from his prison cell to the courthouse to be interrogated by the judge in charge of his case, His Honour Pierre Bouazis. Despite the police's lack of success, the judge was determined to cajole Spaggiari into revealing incriminating information about the heist, and Spaggiari was always happy to waste a judge's time for several hours a week outside his prison cell.

The judge's chambers were located on the third floor of the courthouse, directly above its main entrance. Its main row of windows faced onto the street. The windows were hinged, and about five feet tall. Now, Spaggiari passed all these details on to a cellmate who knew a friend who had a sister who owned a telephone.

For the next three Thursdays, Spaggiari was a little careless in Judge Bouazis's presence. The judge had reason to be pleased with himself.

His manner toward Spaggiari loosened up a little. He became more friendly. He was anxious to keep Spaggiari in his co-operative mood.

On Thursday, March 10, 1977, while once again in the judge's chambers, Spaggiari heard the throaty growl of a motorcycle revving in the street below. It bellowed sharply through several throttle-pulls, then died abruptly. Spaggiari reached into his file-folder and brought out a set of papers.

"I have made some drawings I think you'll be interested in, Your Honour," he said.

The judge glanced at the papers, and his eyes lit up. They were maps of the sewers and the tunnel into the vault – complete with street names, distances, and route markings. He had been trying to trap Spaggiari into divulging this information for weeks. Now they were getting somewhere.

"I'm afraid they fit together in a rather odd way; I'm not much good at drawing maps. Here, I'll show you."

Spaggiari got up and approached the judge's desk. The desk stood beside the window. To his relief, the judge raised no objections. The two guards were out of range at the other end of the chamber. Spaggiari leaned over the judge's shoulder and pointed at several junctions marked with an x.

"This is where we came in, and this . . . is where we got our electricity for the drills . . ."

The judge bent over the drawings.

"And this, here . . . that's the manhole where we hauled in the tanks . . ."

The motorcycle fired up again.

Spaggiari straightened slowly, still talking, still describing. Then, without warning, he lunged for the window. He flipped up its lever, hurled it open, and jumped onto its sill.

The motorcycle below was a black-and-chrome BMW R75/5 with a sleek Craven fairing and elegant matched saddle-bags.

Now that was quality.

"No! No, don't do it!" someone screamed from inside the room.

Spaggiari leaped. His first target was a narrow ledge above the courthouse entrance, about six feet down. From there he aimed for a parked Renault sedan sixteen feet farther down, smashing an eighteen-inch dent into its roof with his boots. He hit the pavement in a paratrooper's roll, bounced back onto his feet, leaped onto the rear seat of the motorcycle, and was whisked away in a roar of engine exhaust and squealing tires.

The motorcycle headed straight down the rue de la Préfecture, cut abruptly into a side street several blocks later, and disappeared into a nearby alley. Neither the driver nor the motorcycle was ever found.

The police never managed to lay another glove on Spaggiari.

He was reportedly sighted several times in Spain and once in Italy, but nothing was ever confirmed.

His old compatriots in Nice had their own reasons for considering South America – probably Brazil or Argentina – the most likely bet. There, after all, a man worth at least $50 million would have little trouble permanently satisfying a penchant for comfort and quality.

Drunk and Disorderly

Yankee Boondoggle #2

In 1978 a police crackdown on drunken driving in New Orleans's French Quarter had been scoring major hits on the patrons of the area's nightclubs and after-hours bars. A particular police target was the notorious Place Pigalle, a noisy watering hole whose regulars had been a constant thorn in the precinct's side. During the crackdown, Pigalle patrons were arrested with such persistence and convicted with such success that the very existence of the nightclub was threatened. Every midnight a police cruiser took up position in the parking lot beside the club, and drunken patrons trying to drive from that lot – or from anywhere within a three-block radius – were regularly picked off like sitting ducks.

One night, at two o'clock in the morning, a man looking considerably the worse for wear stumbled out of the club's front door, fell against a lamp standard, struggled back onto his feet, and made rather indirectly for the parking lot beside the club. Oblivious to the police cruiser, he staggered to his car, spent at least five minutes extracting his ignition key from his pocket, and another five trying to aim it into the correct little hole. He finally drove off in a spray of gravel, weaving from side to side.

The patrolman on duty flashed on his headlights and tore off in pursuit. It didn't take him long to catch up with his quarry, but, instead of turning on his flashers and forcing the drunk to the curb, he followed several car-lengths back, videotaping the drunk's driving performance with a portable video camera.

It was a pretty conclusive performance. The car lurched about like a water-filled balloon, veering abruptly from lane to lane, braking suddenly without warning, and sometimes remaining motionless at an intersection through several light changes. When the officer was certain he had all the incriminating footage he needed, he turned on his revolving dome flasher, sounded his siren, and pulled the man over to the curb.

From this point on it was all routine. He checked the man's licence, asked him to step out of his car, demanded to know if he had been drinking alcohol (the answer was a very firm "no"), then informed him that he would have to take a roadside breathalyzer test. The man protested his innocence, but agreed to take the test. He breathed with some difficulty into the little tube – the officer had to help him position it properly several times – and the officer recorded the reading for his mobile log.

It was obviously wrong. It showed a reading of .05, well below the legal breathalyzer limit.

Patiently, the officer explained that the driver still wasn't getting it right. Somehow his breath hadn't reached the breathalyzer's chemicals at the bottom of the tube. They repeated the procedure, the officer making sure that the driver blew harder this time.

The reading was still .05.

Something about this breathalyzer was obviously on the blink. The officer apologized, but informed the driver he'd have to come down to headquarters to be tested on the stationary breathalyzer. The man protested the inconvenience, but eventually acquiesced.

At the station he registered the same score: .05.

It made no sense. The man reeked of alcohol. His words were slurred. Trying to touch his nose with his forefinger, he kept missing it by half an inch. He couldn't walk a straight line. He was obviously, patently drunk.

But they had to let him go. They gave him a twelve-hour roadside suspension, though they all knew they couldn't make it stick if he ignored it.

Which he did.

The next night, a similar scenario occurred outside Pigalle in much the same way. It wasn't the same man, and it happened about half an hour later. But when the police caught up with their culprit — dishevelled, burping, obviously stinko — their breathalyzer registered .03.

The cops spent $1,200 having their breathalyzers checked — the mobiles and the station's table model. They all worked fine.

Two nights later, it was the same story. And now there were reports from other precincts, describing similar experiences. Whatever was going on, it was spreading right across town.

It was the duty officer at Germantown who finally figured it out. He called the French Quarter officers and suggested a remedy.

That night, a police cruiser parked in the lot beside Pigalle in its usual spot. When a drunk staggered out of Pigalle's front door and made for the parking lot, the patrolman waited patiently until the man had climbed into his car, and let him drive off the lot, lurching and weaving. Then he flashed on his headlights and followed in the usual manner. But as he settled in for a leisurely pursuit, he radioed the precinct to let them know he had left the Pigalle. Nine unmarked cruisers immediately headed over to replace him, their sirens and flashers turned off.

They took up unobtrusive positions all around the club. Eight of the patrolmen lay down across their front seats to make their cars look empty. The ninth kept an eye on the nightclub's two doors. Everything looked still and empty; the only sounds were the muffled thuddings of Pigalle's downstairs dance band and the occasional screech of tires.

Suddenly the Pigalle's back door opened and a man poked his head out. He swivelled in all directions, scrutinizing the parking lot and the surrounding area. Satisfied, he opened the door completely and a bright flood of light spilled into the street.

With the light came a wave of Pigalle patrons – laughing, hollering, stumbling, triumphant. They were all roaring drunk, skidding and tottering towards their cars. Engines raced. Gears ground and tires spun. Everybody was in a hurry, which made them all the clumsier. One car bounced off another and stalled. There was a lot of yelling as this was sorted out. Another car ran right over a high curb and smacked its differential against the concrete. Somebody grazed a lamp pole, leaving a strip of moulding behind.

In all the confusion, nobody noticed the additional cars from nearby alleys which stealthily joined this exodus. For a while, in the general stampede, it wasn't even clear who was following whom. It was only after much videotaping, when police emergency flashers suddenly appeared on innocent-looking dashboards and the sirens began to wail, that the realization dawned on nine Pigalle patrons that they'd been well and truly snookered. This time, the breathalyzers worked breathtakingly well.

At the police station later that morning, everyone confessed to what the police had already surmised: every night, instead of being the "designated driver," one of Pigalle's patrons played the "designated drunk," the decoy who would spend the night drinking sodas and would draw off the patrolling police just before closing time. It had worked very well for four days running – so well that the secret had quickly spread to other parts of town. The story in reverse – word of the police's counter-strategy – didn't travel nearly as fast. It was kept out of the papers at police request, and allowed the police to run three more successful stings before the rumour mill finally broke through. All told, twenty-three drunk drivers were arrested and convicted in magistrate's court.

Despite its obviously limited potential, this gambit also proved portable and transferrable. Reports of copycat versions surfaced sporadically in North America throughout the 1970s and 1980s, and the scheme is considered a perennial dodge by police and police academies. In Sydney, Australia, one nightclub even hired a professional actor on behalf of its patrons.

The Man Who
Fell from the Sky

———◆◆◆———

D. B. Cooper – A Modern Fairy Tale

At five o'clock on the Wednesday evening of November 24, 1971, Northwest Airlines flight 305 had just levelled off at thirty thousand feet and was heading due north, en route from Portland, Oregon, towards Seattle, Washington. Onboard were thirty-six passengers, a three-man flight crew, and two stewardesses.

Since the flight was short – under one hour – no food services were scheduled. So it took the man sitting in 15D – a middle-aged black-haired businessman, wearing a dark suit and tinted glasses – several tries to get stewardess Florence Schaffner's attention. When he did, he handed her a folded note. "Please read it," he requested mildly.*

_____

* This and all subsequent quotes are paraphrased from *D. B. Cooper: What Really Happened* by Max Gunther. See "Sources."

Suspecting a message she could well do without – this sort of thing was always happening to stewardesses – Schaffner just pocketed the note. But the man refused to be put off. "Read it," he insisted. Finally Schaffner relented. The note informed her, in hand-printed letters: "I have a bomb in my briefcase. I will require one million dollars* in twenty-dollar bills and four parachutes. These items must be delivered to me at Seattle Airport as soon as we land. If these demands are not met, I will blow up this aircraft."

At first, the flight crew thought it was a joke, and in bad taste, too. In 1971, commercial airline hijackings were still unknown in North America, and no procedures manual offered any advice on how to handle them. But a short, whispered conversation with the man in 15D convinced pilot William Scott that his passenger was not kidding. Giving the pilot a brief glimpse of two red cylinders connected by a tangle of wires inside his briefcase, the man added, "I don't want you to land until the money and the parachutes are ready for pick-up."

Scott radioed Seattle Airport Traffic Control, and SATC called the Seattle police. The SPD called the FBI. A quickly widening net of calls crisscrossed the darkening Pacific Northwest. There were no precedents to fall back on; everybody was flying by the seat of his pants. The buck finally stopped with Northwest Airlines president Donald Nyrop. He made a decision that has since become the operating principle for airline hijackings throughout North America.

"Give him whatever he wants," he ordered.

The events of the next three hours revealed just how carefully D. B. Cooper (the name announced by the FBI) had

---

* For consistency, all dollar amounts in this volume have been adjusted to 1990 values.

planned this caper. His first demand – no landing until the money and the parachutes were ready – gave the authorities no time to mark the money or set up any of their usual boobytraps. The demand for four parachutes, suggesting that one or more airlines personnel might also be forced to use them, kept anyone from sabotaging the chutes.

As flight 305 locked into a holding pattern over Seattle Airport, local police scrambled to gather the money and the parachutes before the plane's fuel ran out. By the time they had everything ready, the Boeing 727 had been circling for almost an hour. It was finally cleared to land at 5:40 p.m.

After letting everyone deplane except the flight crew and one stewardess, Cooper issued instructions that left law-enforcement officials even more impressed. He ordered the air-craft refuelled and then flown at an airspeed of no more than 150 knots and an altitude of no more than ten thousand feet – he had an altimeter strapped to his wrist to verify this – with flaps and landing gear down and the cabin unpressurized. He also ordered the pilot to fly on a vector 23 course (south) to Reno, Nevada.

It didn't take long for the reasons behind these instructions to become clear, either. A ceiling of ten thousand feet was gen-erally accepted as the highest altitude from which a parachutist could safely jump without oxygen. And, of all the commercial jets flown in North America, only a Boeing 727 could fly at 150 knots without stalling. Furthermore, only a 727 had a rear door that could be opened in flight. Finally, a 727's engines were posi-tioned in such a way that neither the door nor the engines posed any danger to an exiting parachutist. Cooper had selected the perfect aircraft for his score.

Back in the air with the money and the parachutes, Cooper waited until the plane had reached ten thousand feet and he was able to assure himself, from the position of the Rockies on his left and the Cascade Mountains on his right, that they were indeed flying down vector 23. Then he ordered everybody into the cockpit.

In the 1970s, a 727's cockpit door had no peephole in it. The flight crew could now no longer see what Cooper was doing. He strapped the money bag to his chest – stuffing into it, as an afterthought, several apples and chocolate bars from the galley – then buckled on one of the parachutes. He unsnapped its ripcord handle, tested the tension, then opened the plane's rear door.

Nobody ever determined precisely when D. B. Cooper jumped. As the plane flew over the Lewis River in southwest Washington, it dipped briefly and had to be trimmed back. Two pursuing F-106 fighter planes from nearby McChord Air Force Base, incapable of flying at much under five hundred knots, spent most of their time overshooting the 727 and circling back. They didn't see a thing. Neither did the pilot of a National Guard helicopter, who couldn't even find the 727 in the low cloud and rain-squalls. Only a small National Guard Lockheed T-33 trainer, already in the air on another mission, managed to intercept the 727 somewhere over Oregon. Its pilot dogged the slow-flying airliner all the way to the Oregon–California border, but saw nothing either.

✦

The reaction of the media – first in the United States, then across the world – was explosive. Newspapers as far away as Japan, Germany, and even the Soviet Union gave the story front-page treatment. In North America, where the "sixties generation" was busily tuning in and dropping out, anyone under thirty automatically rooted for Cooper as a far-out role model. But polls soon showed that the story had also struck a chord among Cooper's own "silent generation," America's sub-urban middle class. To them he seemed an ordinary, non-radical guy who'd somehow managed to find the guts to turn their own secret fantasy into reality: to break out of the rat race, to catapult out of a grey life into pure adventure.

He was Robin Hood, Kool Kat, and The Man in the Grey Flannel Suit all wrapped up into one.

To the obvious delight of many, the FBI was having no luck at all. An artist's conception of Cooper's mug, based on passengers' recollections, turned out to look like anybody and everybody. A Northwest-wide computer search of males named Cooper accomplished little more than making life exceedingly difficult for a two-timing Portland plumber named Derek Barton Cooper who didn't really want to say where he'd been at the time of the hijacking. A search of the entire six-hundred-mile route between Seattle and Reno was clearly out of the question. A barrage of tips, leads, and hunches sizzled briefly and then evaporated. The mystery extortionist had parachuted out of Northwest's airliner and disappeared into thin air.

And then, just when it seemed their investigation had stalled completely, the FBI hit paydirt. Captain William Scott finally mentioned something that had been bothering him ever since the night of the hijacking.

It was the dip, the brief dip as the airliner had flown over the Lewis River in Cowlitz County, Washington. Given the 150,000-pound weight of a Boeing 727, it hardly seemed possible that a 180-pound man could have influenced the flight attitude of such a heavy plane. But when Northwest Airlines staged a re-enactment, pushing a loaded sled off the plane's airstairs during flight, the resulting bob and weave of the airliner confirmed Scott's suspicion. With the help of the 727's

November 24 flight recorder, he was now able to give the FBI a pretty good idea when and where Cooper had jumped.

Within days, a flotilla of airplanes and helicopters from the U.S. Air Force, the National Guard, the U.S. Army, and the Weyerhauser Lumber Company homed in on Washington's Cowlitz and Clark counties. Wave after wave of them criss-crossed the area's vast evergreen forests, looking, in the words of one pilot, "for a parachute or a hole." An early sighting of what appeared to be a parachute hanging in a large evergreen turned out to be just a deflated weather balloon. A large piece of orange fabric in a meadow proved to be a tarp-covered teepee. Several futile weeks later an early snowfall brought the operation to a halt, but the following spring, three hundred army troops from Fort Lewis and a crowd of paid civilian volunteers converged on the area again.

✦

Had they known how close they came to catching their quarry on both occasions, they'd probably have jumped out of their airplanes themselves. Captain Scott's suspicions and calculations had been remarkably accurate. Cooper had indeed parachuted out of the 727 over Clark County near the Lewis River, and had drifted downwind towards a small town whose lights were the first thing he saw when he sank beneath the area's heavy cloud cover. He had steered towards those lights.

So far, everything had gone exactly as planned. After landing, Cooper intended to bury the parachute and his suit jacket. The heavy sweater he was wearing underneath would blend in more readily in a logging town. The backpack containing the money wouldn't raise an eyebrow in backpacking country. He had travelled the area and had made sure about things like that.

His landing, however, didn't go exactly as planned. Distracted by the distant lights, he didn't realize he was almost down until an evergreen branch flashed by on his left. By then it was too late to position himself for a five-point rolling landing. He hit the ground with an undignified yelp and felt a sharp stab of pain sear through his ankle. His face ploughed into a thick mattress of wet leaves, plugging his nose and mouth.

He spat twigs and leaves and then lay still for a while, just listening. All he could hear was the wind in the evergreens, and gurgling water.

The pain in his ankle felt serious. The shin and the femur ached, too. He sat up, pulled in the chute, and rolled it up. It was too dark to tackle anything more that night. He covered himself with the chute and tried to sleep, to ignore the pain and the cold.

All things considered, there was very little evidence that D. B. Cooper had just fallen out of the sky into a modern fairy tale.

The next morning provided even less evidence for this fact. The wind and rain had increased, and the pain in his ankle was excruciating. His carefully calculated plan was unravelling fast. He cut himself a walking stick, stuffed a thick wad of bills into his underwear, buried both the parachute and the money-filled backpack, and struggled off in the direction of the town.

He made it only as far as a small cabin on the town's outskirts. Each step was sending an explosion of pain through his leg. He dragged himself into a small toolshed at the edge of the cabin's lawn and barely managed to close the door. Then he passed out.

✦

Clara (the name she used to identify herself years later) was a perfectly capable, presentable, round-faced, medium tall, bespectacled woman in her thirties.

That wasn't, however, her own opinion of herself. Her self-doubts had been encouraged by her family – particularly her mother and her two older brothers – who had never outgrown the habit of treating Clara as a baby. Throughout her life, their overprotective reactions to every opportunity – a scholarship from a distant college, the offer of work and a shared apartment in New York from a high-school girl friend – had closed door after door. Born in Longview, Washington, not far from the Lewis River in Cowlitz County, she had always dreamed of escaping the Northwest's logging mentality, but had settled instead for a loveless marriage and a job as a secretary. The marriage had lasted less than five years.

In September 1971, an uncle who owned a cabin on the Lewis River, and who was about to spend a year overseas, began looking for someone to take care of his cabin and his dog. Clara volunteered. She felt in a rut; she needed some quiet to sort things out. The uncle sympathized. Clara quit her job and moved into the cabin with the dog.

On the morning of November 26, the dog found the tool-shed out back more than usually exciting. Clara assumed he had cornered a skunk, or maybe a raccoon.

Instead, she found a dark-eyed, dark-suited stranger lying on the floor, in obvious pain. He had regained consciousness only moments before.

✦

At this point, the story could have gone in several directions. A panicked call to the local sheriff. A short, successful manhunt through the nearby bush.

But Clara didn't call the sheriff. There was something about this man – his quiet, courteous manner, his calm, if somewhat evasive, replies – that struck a chord in her. Instead, she made him some tea and drove him to the local doctor.

After his broken ankle had been splinted, and after she'd told the doctor he was a visiting cousin, she stared (by her own account) for a long time into the mirror of the doctor's washroom, grimacing at herself with raised eyebrows and head-shaking reproof. Then she took him back to her cabin.

He said his name was Paul Cotton, though she doubted that. He was obviously on the run from something, and he admitted as much, mumbling vaguely about bad debts. It wasn't until a day or two later, after they'd become more comfortable with one another and she'd told him all about herself, that he began to tell her what she instinctively believed to be his real story. About his childhood in southern Ontario, his youth in New Jersey, and his average, standard, middle-class life: a stint in the U.S. Army as a paratrooper, C + -level college grades, an uninspired marriage, a run-of-the-mill salesman's job, a suburban existence, his eventual decision to chuck it all. They were obviously very similar.

When the truth finally dawned on her – she did, after all, watch television – she asked him point-blank, before she could reconsider: "Are you the hijacker? The man they're calling D. B. Cooper?"

He didn't try to deny it. He just nodded.

"Oh, Lord," Clara said, dropping her head into her hands. "What do we do now?"

He didn't move from the couch where she'd positioned him with his ankle propped up on an adjacent coffee table. His voice remained neutral and calm.

"I guess that's up to you, Clara."

✦

What Clara did was fall in love with Cotton. And he with her. It didn't happen overnight, but it happened more quickly than either of them had bargained for. Within several weeks they were living as man and wife.

It may have been a relationship of convenience, but it felt very right. They fit together like a dovetail joint. His unoppressive, supportive presence stiffened her backbone and helped her disentangle herself from her family's control. Her quiet understanding and admiration for his daring and ingenuity – qualities no one had ever appreciated in him before – made him feel a lot less average. And, though neither admitted it in so many words, they both enjoyed as well as feared the dangerous adventure into which they'd suddenly climbed.

For the danger was becoming very real. Within days of Cotton's arrival, the area was swarming with aircraft and FBI agents. Local papers and local talk seemed concerned with little else. On her brief, unavoidable excursions into town for groceries, Clara's tendency to paranoia received a vigorous fanning. Every night the evening news included increasingly optimistic FBI updates. The baying of the wolves was coming closer and closer.

But then the snow began to fall, and everything quietened. First the airplanes left, and then the FBI. After a Christmas spent in contented seclusion, the two finally decided to retrieve the money that was still buried out in the bush. It took them less than two hours to trudge the distance it had taken Paul a full day to cover on his wounded ankle two months before.

But when they reached the right place, the money was gone.

At first Clara thought Paul had simply lost his bearings. In the bush, with new snow everywhere, that was easy to do. But after a little digging, Paul found the parachute. It was exactly where he remembered burying it.

Sitting on a log, dejected after several more hours of futile searching, the two ate sandwiches and tried to figure it out. The most likely explanation was that someone had somehow stumbled onto the money and carried it off. The thief had had his booty stolen. It was a moral outcome one couldn't really argue with, but that made it no less depressing. After all that risk and ingenuity.

A raccoon sniffing around the various holes they had dug suddenly gave Paul a brainwave. The apples and the chocolate bars – he had left them in the bag with the money. And raccoons always washed their food. There might be a connection. They scrambled off their log and headed for the nearby creek.

It took them several tries, but they finally found the money. Not all of it, however. The bag had been chewed open and only some of the banknotes were still inside. They discovered others scattered under the snow, sodden and muddy. Altogether they recovered $516,000, plus the $82,000 Paul had taken earlier – a total of $598,000.

So they were rich – but they couldn't use the money. The FBI had published the bills' serial numbers, and while few tellers paid much attention to such lists, the possibility was always there. Meanwhile, Clara's meagre savings were dwindling fast. They were rich but broke, with over half a million dollars going to waste in Clara's attic.

They decided to head for New York City. In that huge place, they felt sure they could sneak the money back into circulation, slowly and carefully. Paul gathered all the evidence they had dug up – the parachute, his suit jacket, the money bag – and burned them in the cabin's fireplace. Clara sold her car and made arrangements for a neighbour to take care of the dog. She told her family she was going to Texas, but she left no forwarding address. They left from Portland in mid-March 1972, barely a week before the FBI descended on Cowlitz and Clark counties once again, to conduct the biggest ground search and dragnet operation the area had ever seen.

In New York, the lovebirds were astonished to discover that going underground wasn't going to be as easy as they'd thought. Crossing Long Island Park soon after their arrival, on their way to several banks to open accounts with a modest handful of Paul's banknotes, they passed a teenager wearing a T-shirt reading: "D. B. COOPER, WHERE ARE YOU?" Not long after, ballad singer Tom Bresh wrote a popular song about the hijacking that played on the radio for months. And soon after that, the FBI circulated a new composite drawing of Cooper, making him look heavier, with thicker hair. Every few months, it seemed, something or someone kept reviving the story. And while the steadily growing Cooper legend wasn't hurting Paul's ego, it wasn't helping him launder his money, either.

By 1975, virtually all of the money was still locked in its suitcase – and it looked as if it might just stay there forever. The FBI had recently gone to court to charge "John Doe, a.k.a. D. B. Cooper" with air piracy, a tactic law-enforcement agencies commonly used to wipe out the usual five-year statute of limitations. Both Clara and Paul had found jobs, and their combined incomes were now more than sufficient for everyday living expenses. But they were still treading water, at least economically, constantly tantalized and mocked by a suitcaseful of money that could catapult them into fairyland if they could just figure out how to break its spell.

In 1976, Paul finally figured it out. A friend who had just returned from Reno expressed amazement at how much cash people threw around in casinos. On a business trip to Nevada later that year, Paul took along a wad of bills, bought $100,000 worth of chips, gambled briefly (winning $500), then cashed out.

It worked like a charm. Over the next few years, both Paul and Clara made several trips to Las Vegas, Atlantic City, and back to Reno. Each time, they laundered another bundle of bills, and neither ever encountered any problems.

The spell on the hijack ransom had finally been broken.

Now their fairy tale really began to blossom. They were suddenly able to buy a house on Long Island, in a community which quickly warmed to them. To their surprise, they found themselves becoming popular. What neither had been able to become individually, they now became successfully together. Their circle of friends grew. They joined a country club. Their home became a focal point for the community.

Their own relationship kept growing stronger, too. They discovered a capacity for romance they'd only suspected in themselves. Paul bought Clara a lot of flowers and chocolates. They both enjoyed reading and travel. They were contented in their jobs, and both received several promotions. Clara's paranoia was fading fast . . .

And that's how it should have ended – both living happily ever after – by all the rules of fairyland. But a shadow drifted over their lives in late 1980, when a personnel clerk discovered that Paul's college degree had been faked.

Since Paul couldn't provide the details about the legitimate college degree he'd earned under his birth name, he was stuck. Initially, because he was well liked and his work had always been exemplary, Paul was allowed to stay, but a second discovery – that virtually *all* the information in his personnel file had been faked – proved too much for the company to handle. He was let go without the usual letters of reference.

This made it impossible for Paul to find another job. Though he kept at it diligently, sending résumés and applications to hundreds of companies, the lack of a demonstrable track record proved insurmountable. Of course, he didn't need the money. He could have retired on the spot, but he belonged to a generation whose self-respect was inextricably tied to a paying job. He became dejected, then morose.

And then one day Clara noticed an abrupt change in Paul. A change not necessarily for the worse – he was suddenly happier, more purposeful – but she couldn't see any obvious reason for it. He wasn't having any more luck finding a job than before.

It wasn't long before she discovered he was spending his days at La Guardia Airport. He made no effort to deny it when she confronted him. He'd been checking out the planes, he admitted, "just watching all the planes."

Her heart sank. She asked him anxiously if he was going to try it again. He didn't deny that either. She saw disaster looming, and there was nothing she could do about it.

She knew Paul Cotton – or whatever his name was – well enough by now.

But Paul Cotton never got the chance to hijack another airliner.

A few weeks later he died of a heart attack.

Some years after that, Clara – or whatever *her* name was – still mourning the loss of the most wonderful man in the world, decided to tell their story as a sort of monument to his memory. She contacted the New York journalist Max Gunther, whose articles Paul had always enjoyed.

Gunther questioned Clara thoroughly. It didn't take him long to realize that her story was probably true. She knew many details that had never been publicized by the FBI. She knew, for example, that the name on the air ticket had not been D. B. Cooper, but rather Dan Cooper. She knew exactly what he'd been wearing on the night of November 24, 1971, and was able to corroborate or correct many other facts the FBI had either misreported or misunderstood. It all fit together – like a dovetail joint.

Clara never revealed her real name, or the name of the man she called Paul Cotton. The FBI have never discovered it either. But the impact of "D. B. Cooper" on modern air travel has been profound enough to make that detail largely irrelevant. The Cooper hijacking sparked the development of the plethora of sophisticated security devices and procedures that virtually seal up the world's airports today. The Cooper hijacking caused the Boeing Aircraft Company to modify its 727, so that its rear door can no longer be opened in flight and its cockpit door has a peephole.

No one has ever successfully replicated Cooper's caper. A year later, in 1972, three others tried, but, unaware of Boeing's modifications, all failed. The FBI shot all three.

Virtual Whiplash

Yankee Boondoggle #3

On March 17, 1989, a commuter bus belonging to the Orange, Newark & Elizabeth Bus Company of New Jersey collided with a passenger sedan belonging to New Jersey resident Douglas Mortimer. The fender-bender occurred at low speed during heavy commuter traffic and none of the twenty-three passengers on the bus seemed injured – and neither did Douglas Mortimer, who ruefully exchanged insurance information with the bus driver and then shook hands. Both the bus and the car continued on under their own power.

Nevertheless, by April 7, three weeks later, the O.N.E. Bus Company had received severe-injury claims from thirty-seven passengers – fourteen more than had been on the bus – plus Douglas Mortimer *and* two men who claimed their car had been hit by the bus after it collided with Mortimer's sedan. Total demands by all claimants exceeded a million dollars.

It was a day like most other days for the O.N.E. Bus Company. This sort of thing had become so common that its comptroller was almost inured to the phenomenon. That's just what the company's high insurance premiums – which had grown during the past six years from $9,000 to $23,000 annually per bus – were for: to protect it against the increasingly ridiculous claims of Americans who found that taking an insurance company to court could be a profitable pastime. Taking *anybody* to court for *anything* was becoming the latest form of casino gambling – but with far better odds. The settlements were becoming so lucrative, one might be forgiven for *hoping* to get into an accident.

The comptroller sighed, and gathered up the claims to send on to the New Jersey Insurance Department.

That "accident" proved to be the last straw for New Jersey's insurance commissioner Samuel Fortunato. To convince both law-enforcement and court officials that fake insurance claims were costing insurance companies $4 billion every year, he set up a sting operation that proceeded, over the next three years, to "crash" a total of ten buses in carefully staged, videotaped circumstances, permitting investigators to monitor all aspects of the accidents with legally compelling accuracy.

What they found astonished even the police and insurance investigators.

The first accident was staged in March 1990, in East Orange, New Jersey. An ordinary-looking bus carrying fifteen passengers (all actors who were in on the sting) was rear-ended by a car (also in on the sting) travelling less than ten miles per hour.

No sooner had the crash occurred and the bus driver stepped out to speak to the car's driver than *seventeen additional people* scrambled aboard through the open door, posing as passengers who had been hurt in the crash. They slid to the floor, moaned in pain, and massaged their necks and shoulders. When police arrived, they demanded to be taken to hospital by ambulance – the courts, apparently, took ambulance-involved claims more seriously – and insisted on being carried off the bus on stretchers. When all the paperwork was in, every one of them had filed large injury claims – *as had two others who hadn't even been on the bus*, neither before nor after the accident. They'd merely heard about it and "gave it a shot."

Subsequent crashes produced evidence of even-more-sophisticated swindles. Professional accident victims with police-band radios listened in on police reports and hurried out to the scenes of accidents as soon as they were reported. Bus passengers frequently found themselves swarmed by "runners," flacks in the employ of crooked lawyers or doctors, who flooded onto the buses to lecture passengers on how to make claims, what to claim for, and whom to hire to pursue the claims. They handed out business cards, telephone numbers, and leaflets containing instructions on how to proceed with a claim. If the police hadn't yet arrived, these runners often dropped their promotional efforts and "became" passengers themselves.

Every staged crash seemed to bring more swindlers out of the woodwork. The actors who'd been hired to impersonate passengers reported that, when they gave out their personal telephone numbers, they were inundated with phone calls from doctors and lawyers pressuring them – often offering bribes – to make fake claims and accept phoney treatments. When the actors agreed, the lawyers routinely exaggerated their claims and also had no compunction about defending "passengers" they knew hadn't been anywhere near the accident. The doctors also padded their bills, frequently doubling or trebling the number of actual treatments performed – treatments that were generally unnecessary in the first place – and adding numerous fake tests and procedures. Their bills generally ranged between $4,500 and $6,000 per case.

Crooked policemen proved willing to add the names of fake accident victims to their police reports for a bribe or a percentage of the claims take. Ambulance drivers alerted professional accident victims to accident locations for a cash payment or a percentage: some would even pick them up on the way to or from the accident scene.

The action became so competitive in some neighbourhoods that just the *sound* of a crash unleashed a wave of claims. One bus driver reported that, when he stopped to assist the drivers of two non-sting vehicles that had collided *behind* his bus, twenty-seven passengers who assumed from the sound of crunching metal that the bus had been involved as well, promptly filed injury claims. The bus hadn't even been touched.

All told, 107 people were charged in the New Jersey sting operation, including doctors, lawyers, policemen, runners, and ninety-seven fake passengers. Most were convicted. But the problem hasn't gone away. In fact, insurance spokespeople claim it's still growing. Similar reports continue to surface all over the United States, and will undoubtedly continue to do so, as long as U.S. courts make playing claims poker the enormously profitable pastime it has become.

Hitler for Sale

―――――◆―◆――――――

The Hitler Diaries Fiasco

Gerd Heidemann was in a fix.

The forty-four-year-old reporter for the German magazine *Stern* had just broken up with his third wife. His house, a modest bungalow in a Hamburg suburb, was mortgaged to the hilt. He had debts of over $100,000,* was behind on his payments, and overdue on the submission of a book he'd contracted to write three years earlier, in 1973.

And now this.

"This" was the sorry hulk of a yacht presently moored in a Hamburg marina with a "For Sale" sign on her foredeck: the

―――――――

* For consistency, all dollar amounts in this volume have been adjusted to 1990 values.

Carin II, which was supposed to have solved all of Heidemann's money troubles in one tidy transaction.

It wasn't the *Carin II*'s looks he'd been counting on to accomplish this financial miracle. It was her pedigree.

In 1937, the eighty-five-foot yacht had constituted the pinnacle of Germany's marine technology. She had been built for the commander-in-chief of Germany's Luftwaffe, Reichsmarschall Hermann Goering. After the war and Goering's death, she had been impounded by Field Marshal Montgomery and presented to Britain's Royal Family. They, in turn, had rechristened her the *Royal Albert*. In 1960, after a decade's service in the British Rhine flotilla, she'd been returned to Goering's second wife and widow by Queen Elizabeth herself.

After that, her genealogy had taken a decided nose-dive.

When Heidemann found her, in 1973, she was lying low in the water at an industrial wharf in Bonn. Her decks were cracked and peeling, her hull leaked, only one of her three engines worked, and she was barely seaworthy. Her current owner, a printing-shop proprietor, was willing to dump her for $150,000.

Heidemann knew nothing about boats, but he knew about the strong and perennial world-wide market for Third Reich memorabilia. His research for historical *Stern* articles had taken him through many German antique shops, and he knew about the dozens of catalogues circulating throughout the Western world, offering everything from locks of Eva Braun's hair to Martin Bormann's pyjamas. The prices were staggering, and the greatest demand for Nazi relics came from the United States.

With a few quick patches and a gallon or two of paint, Heidemann calculated, he could make a fortune selling this yacht to some collector of Nazi relics. At least a million. Maybe two. She was a steal at $150,000.

He had hurried back to Hamburg and mortgaged his house to raise the money. Three weeks later, a sailor friend had helped him sail the *Carin II* from Bonn to a Hamburg drydock. Despite using only inland waterways and running her pumps nonstop, they'd barely made it.

For a couple of weeks, Heidemann was on top of the world. A few patches and a bit of paint. Man, what a find. A million dollars' profit. Maybe twice that much. Maybe three times that much. Some of those Texan collectors would pay almost anything. He'd heard of Himmler's toothbrush going for $25,000. He'd seen Goebbels's false teeth advertised for $100,000. One of Hitler's monogrammed spoons had recently pulled down something like $7,000.

Then the shipyard's estimates arrived.

Just to repair the hull was going to cost $350,000.

Replacing the two inoperative engines would cost $135,000.

Restoring the superstructure would cost about $750,000.

Modern navigational gear would cost another $125,000.

Add another $50,000 for various odds and ends.

Sum total: $1,410,000.

Heidemann felt a distinct urge to shoot himself.

Over the next six months, he tried every potential solution he could think of. He tried to mortgage the yacht. He tried to sell partnerships in her. He tried to sell her just as she was – in drydock. He listed her with Jakob Tiefenthaeler, a well-known Nazi-memorabilia broker, at $1,500,000. No takers. $1,000,000. Nothing. $750,000. Not a twitch. $500,000. $250,000. Not even a raised eyebrow.

It was clear that the *Carin II* would have to be seaworthy before she was sellable at all. And that would mean, at the very least, caulking her hull.

At this point, Heidemann got a bit of a break. After weeks of trying, he finally managed to get his boss, the founding publisher of *Stern* magazine, to have a look at his historical relic.

Henri Nannen was intrigued. His magazine peddled a populist mix of scandal, crime, sex, consumerism, and human interest. A series of features on some of the old Nazi war criminals, with reminiscences by some of Hitler's closest subordinates, would probably sell well on the newsstands. He concluded an agreement with Heidemann, giving him an immediate $75,000 advance to produce such a series, using the *Carin II* as a drawing card. He calculated – correctly as it turned out – that Goering's old yacht would attract old Nazis like moths to a yellow light bulb.

Relieved, Heidemann phoned the drydock and ordered the caulking to begin.

✦

It wasn't long before Heidemann's research into the *Carin II*'s history led him to Goering's daughter Edda. They began an affair. She introduced him to other Nazis: ss General Wilhelm Mohnke, the last commander of the Reich Chancellery before the Russians overwhelmed it; ss General Karl Wolff, the oldest surviving Nazi general. Soon dozens of other Nazis began to gravitate to Goering's old yacht, too. It became an unofficial Nazi clubhouse. Heidemann poured the whisky, handed around sandwiches, and kept his tape recorder running.

It was at one such gathering, late in 1977, that General Mohnke gave Heidemann a copy of *The Catacombs*, an account of Hitler's last days by *Newsweek* reporter James P. O'Donnell.

Though the book was in most respects identical to dozens of similar works on that topic, it did contain a story Heidemann hadn't heard before. Sergeant Rochus Misch, the switchboard operator for the Fuehrer-Bunker, reported that he'd climbed out of the bunker for a smoke on the afternoon of April 20, 1945, Hitler's birthday, to find two men, Sergeant Wilhelm Arndt and a soldier named Fehrs, manhandling ten large metal trunks onto a flatbed truck.

The trunks were being transported to a nearby airport as part of Operation Seraglio, the evacuation of Hitler's papers, valuables, and personal property from Berlin. They were loaded onto two Luftwaffe aircraft, one piloted by a Sergeant Dietrich Schultze and the other by a Major Friedrich Gundlfinger. The two planes took off shortly before dawn, after repeated Allied air raids, with Schultze choosing to hide as much as possible inside a meagre cloud cover, while Gundlfinger stayed as close to the ground as his big Junkers 352 transport could handle.

Both tactics failed, although Schultze managed to reach Prague – then still under German control – before his punctured fuel line gave way. Gundlfinger, however, got only as far as the Heidenholz Forest, near the Czech border. A roving U.S. fighter scored a direct hit and Gundlfinger's plane burst into flames, ploughing into the ground just outside the village of Boernersdorf (eventually in East Germany). The intense heat and exploding ammunition kept villagers from trying to rescue its passengers, among whom was Wilhelm Arndt.

When ss General Hans Baur informed Hitler of the crash, Hitler reacted with unexpected emotion. He became, Baur remembered, very pale, and exclaimed in an anguished voice: "In that plane were all my private archives; everything I'd intended as a testament to posterity. It's a catastrophe!"

Intrigued, O'Donnell had tracked down and interviewed several of Hitler's personal secretaries. All of them corroborated the story. They suggested that the trunks had probably contained the verbatim transcripts of Hitler's military conferences at the Fuehrer-Bunker, which Hitler had ordered collected and saved for future historical research. They were less unanimous about whether the trunks might also have contained Hitler's more personal writings, or the transcripts of his famous "table talks" – documents known to have been prepared but never found after the Nazi surrender in Berlin. O'Donnell wrapped up his account with a teaser:

> As all police reporters know, documents have a way of surviving crashes in which humans are cremated. While even metal melts, a book or a notebook does not burn easily, above all when packed tightly into a container excluding oxygen. Paper in bulk tends rather to char at the edges. . . . One is left with the nagging thought that some Bavarian hayloft, chicken coop, or even pigsty may well have been waterproofed and insulated with millions of words of the Fuehrer's unpublished, ineffable utterances, simply hauled away at dawn as loot from a burning German transport plane.

Gerd Heidemann found that part particularly fascinating.

If a person could get his hands on something as electrifying as Hitler's personal writings, that person would never have to worry about money problems again.

A book of Hitler's personal journals would constitute the publishing coup of the century.

✦

"True seekers know," the French writer La Rochefoucault once said, "that once a search has commenced, clues become unavoidable."

In December 1980, Heidemann received an excited call from Tiefenthaeler.

No, he didn't have a buyer for the *Carin II*. But he had something even better. He had just examined the Third Reich collection of a wealthy Stuttgart engineer named Fritz Stiefel. And one of Stiefel's most prized possessions, about which he'd sworn Tiefenthaeler to absolute secrecy, had turned out to be a volume of Hitler's personal diaries. It had apparently been rescued from the wreckage of Gundlfinger's plane in 1945.

Every journalistic cell in Heidemann's body went on full red alert.

Less than a week later, he was on Stiefel's doorstep. His purpose, ostensibly, was to invite Stiefel to become a shareholder in the *Carin II*. Failing that – and Stiefel didn't seem interested – Heidemann wondered if he might be permitted a glance at the Hitler diary. He'd recently heard about it from a mutual friend.

Stiefel was startled by the request, and not particularly pleased. But eventually he reluctantly gave in. He led Heidemann to a large steel door, emblazoned with a sign that warned BEWARE. HIGH VOLTAGE. LETHAL DANGER, and disarmed the alarm system.

Inside a large, windowless room, Heidemann found a virtual warehouse of Third Reich relics. Row upon row of expensive, softly lit cabinets contained Nazi uniforms, Swastika flags, Nazi books, paintings, drawings, and military decorations. There were weapons, official documents, proclamations, and posters. There were concentration-camp artefacts, an exhibit of porcelain made by Auschwitz inmates, and an array of personal possessions that had belonged to many of the Third Reich's highest-ranking officials.

It had to be one of the most extensive Nazi collections in all of Germany.

Then Stiefel handed Heidemann the Hitler diary. It was a black-covered, lined notebook, roughly nine-by-twelve inches in size and about one hundred pages long. Some of the pages were filled with writing, some were only half-filled, and some were blank. Some of the writing was in pencil, some in ink. Many of the pages were initialled with Hitler's signature in the lower right-hand corner. The writing itself was in Gothic German script, a script that hadn't been taught in Germany since the Second World War.

Heidemann tried hard to suppress his excitement. Where had the diary come from? How much had it cost? Had it been proven authentic? Were there any more of them to be had?

Stiefel explained that this volume was part of a much larger body of material that had been rescued from the wreck of Gundlfinger's plane near Boernersdorf. His source, he said, was a Stuttgart antique dealer, Konrad Kujau, who'd been acquiring Nazi artefacts through his brother, a high-ranking general in the East German army. He said he'd been told there were another twenty-six volumes available – each one covering a six-month period.

◆

To Heidemann's astonishment, not everyone at *Stern* – nor among the regulars on the *Carin II* – proved as ecstatic about this news as he.

After four years of listening to Heidemann's endless Third

Reich reports, Henri Nannen, his publisher at *Stern*, had "had about as much of this Nazi shit as I can take."*

Edda Goering recalled that Hitler had always hated writing in his own hand; he'd preferred dictating. It seemed to her unlikely that these "diaries" could be genuine.

Generals Mohnke and Wolff declared the idea impossible. They'd spent a lot of time in the Fuehrer's company, and felt he'd never have had the time to keep a diary.

But the executives of Gruner and Jahr (*Stern*'s owners) and the gigantic publishing firm of Bertelsmann AG (Gruner and Jahr's owners) were definitely tantalized. They could see enormous commercial potential in Heidemann's report. They wanted to hear more.

Heidemann already had more. Right after his visit to Stiefel he'd applied for permission to travel to Boernersdorf in East Germany, ostensibly to search for the remains of a relative who had died in the Junkers 352 crash. He'd found the crash site exactly where he'd been told it would be by the Wehrmacht Information Office. He'd found the marked graves of Gundlfinger and Wilhelm Arndt nearby. He'd tracked down relatives of the crash victims and discovered the astonishing fact that at least two of the plane's passengers had survived. Finally, relatives of passengers who had died had showed him a variety of wallets and other identifying documents the Luftwaffe had returned to them after the crash.

It was incontestable proof that papers of various kinds *had* survived that crash.

Buttressed by this report, Gruner and Jahr executives

---

* This and subsequent quotes are taken from *Selling Hitler: Story of the Hitler Diaries* by Robert Harris. See "Sources."

decided to go for broke. They swore all involved principals to total secrecy. They instructed Heidemann to find the Stuttgart antique dealer. They agreed to offer this man – through the agency of *Stern* magazine – the sum of 5 million Deutschmarks (just under $2.5 million) for the twenty-six-volume set of Hitler's diaries.

✦

The $2.5-million offer, passed on via Tiefenthaeler, proved sufficiently enticing to flush Konrad Kujau out of the woodwork.

Short, squat, bald, and (in Heidemann's private estimation) "intellectually limited," the Stuttgart antique dealer had been born to an impoverished, fanatically pro-Nazi family in Loebau (eventually East Germany), in 1938. He'd spent most of his youth in foster homes, had left school at age sixteen, and, after several years of temporary jobs and arrests for petty crimes, had escaped to the West to improve his fortunes.

They hadn't significantly improved. Once again he'd drifted from job to dead-end job, waiting on tables, bartending, loading freight. In 1962 he'd managed to better himself a little by starting up the Pelican Dance Bar in rented premises on the outskirts of Stuttgart, but the bar had gone broke within a year. Then he and his common-law wife, Edith, had founded a window-washing firm.

The firm had made some money, but Kujau had found window-washing a tad repetitious. Then someone told him about the growing Western market for Nazi memorabilia, much of which was being sold out of East Germany for Western currencies. Kujau found this business much more to his liking. He had plenty of contacts in East Germany – including his own brother – who were willing to smuggle artefacts across the border, and the profit margins were astonishing. Over the following decade he established an impressive network for both the acquisition and selling of Nazi relics.

Kujau's speciality became paintings and documents. He had a remarkable nose for them. What Hitler had lacked in quality he'd apparently made up in quantity, because Kujau managed to unearth hundreds of his paintings and drawings. He claimed to have found the original manuscript of *Mein Kampf*. He offered for sale unpublished manuscript copies of some of Hitler's earliest poems – awful doggerel – and the text of an opera, *Wieland the Blacksmith*, which Hitler had co-authored with his boyhood friend August Kubizek in his early twenties.

Heidemann was amazed and fascinated.

With respect to the Hitler diaries, however, Kujau sounded dubious. He told Heidemann that he normally dealt only with private collectors. There were laws in both East and West Germany prohibiting the dissemination of Nazi propaganda, and those laws cast a wide net. Publication of the Hitler diaries by a widely distributed magazine like *Stern* might well endanger careers and – in East Germany at least – actual lives.

Then why not leave *Stern* out of the deal completely, Heidemann suggested. You sell the diaries directly, and only, to me.

Kujau hummed and hawed. But, after much cajoling, he softened up a little. He stressed, however, that under no circumstances – and this was totally non-negotiable – was his identity ever to be divulged to anyone. Under any circumstances. If Heidemann couldn't guarantee this, there was no point in talking further. Both his and Heidemann's lives would be at risk if this condition was ever breached. There were people involved in this business, Kujau warned, who had "absolutely no sense of humour."

Heidemann promised that his lips would be permanently and unconditionally sealed. As a further inducement, he offered Kujau one of Goering's SS uniforms, which had come with the yacht.

Now it was Kujau's turn to salivate. As it happened, he already owned the uniforms of Hitler, Himmler, and Rommel – but not of Goering. The bargaining climate improved significantly.

In the end, Kujau agreed to pass Heidemann off to his brother as a private Swiss collector. Of course, that meant no deals with anyone but Heidemann himself. No other partners. No middlemen.

Heidemann had no problem going along with that stipulation. It actually suited him just fine.

✦

On Wednesday, January 28, 1981, Gerd Heidemann showed up at Konrad Kujau's business premises on Stuttgart's Aspergstrasse with a suitcase stuffed full of cash. It was, he explained, a "down payment" on the Hitler diaries.

Three weeks later, on Tuesday, February 17, 1981, Kujau climbed aboard the *Carin II* to deliver the first three volumes of the diaries. The rest, he informed Heidemann, would be arriving from East Germany in small packets on a monthly basis, hidden in the backs of pianos. Pianos were a major export product of East Germany.

Next morning, Wednesday, February 18, the five executives who now formed the steering committee of the most secretive publishing project in Gruner and Jahr's history, gathered in the managing director's offices to receive the first Hitler diaries.

It was a moment, Heidemann later recalled, of almost religious solemnity.

As they passed the slightly battered, black-covered volumes reverently from hand to hand, two rather important facts became evident.

One: they were holding in their hands a document that, in less than a year, would probably set the whole world on its ear, a document that might well require a complete reassessment of Western history from 1935 to the present; and

Two: they were all – with the single exception of Gerd Heidemann – incapable of reading a word of it.

Fact number two, the result of Hitler's Gothic-script handwriting, which they were all too young to have learned in school, was casually sidestepped by having Heidemann read various excerpts out loud.

Fact number one became clear from the startling excerpts themselves – excerpts that indicated (for example) that Hitler had known of Deputy Fuehrer Rudolf Hess's quixotic 1941 mission to England *before* it had actually happened.

As one of the executives succinctly put it: "Fasten your seatbelts, gentlemen!"

✦

The arresting excerpts from the first Hitler diaries convinced Gruner and Jahr's executives to take radical measures to protect their extraordinary find.

First, they decided to secure the entire set at all costs. In view of Heidemann's threat that his East German source would immediately cease further deliveries if word of the diaries leaked out, this meant that no one – no historians, no forensic experts, and no handwriting analysts – would be permitted to see the diaries until the complete set was safely in Gruner and Jahr's vault.

Second, the project was given a code name, "The Green Vault," and completely divorced from the company's regular publishing program. In fact, separate offices were set up for it in another part of the city.

Third, a contract was negotiated with Heidemann, authorizing him to pay his source the sum of $100,000 for each volume of the diaries. A further contract gave Heidemann a 6-per-cent-to-9-per-cent graduated royalty on the cover price of the anticipated book (expected sales in the order of five million copies) plus a whopping 36 per cent of all syndication rights. Finally, Heidemann was given an immediate non-refundable advance of $300,000, a company Mercedes, and a fully paid release from all other assignments for two years.

There was no doubt in anyone's mind that the Hitler diaries were going to make everyone involved in their publication very, very rich.

✦

From February 1981, Kujau and Heidemann developed a routine that remained largely unchanged during the two-year period over which the Hitler diaries were delivered.

Kujau would call Heidemann to report the arrival of another package of diaries.

Heidemann alerted Gruner and Jahr executive Wilfried Sorge, who alerted the company's treasurer.

The treasurer called the company's bank and made an appointment to pick up between $100,000 and $200,000 in used 500-and 1,000-Deutschmark bills.

The money was bundled into a briefcase and delivered to Heidemann.

Everyone talked to each other in code. The record of these transactions was kept to a minimum, and also written in code.

Heidemann was not required to document his expenditures with receipts, reports, or explanations of any kind.

From February until mid-May, 1981, the diaries arrived in packages of one or two every several weeks.

✦

On June 1, 1981, following the delivery of the twelfth diary, Heidemann announced a price increase. His "source" was now demanding $125,000 per volume – to cover increased bribery demands from his customs contact.

Heidemann's bosses weren't so much bothered by the increased price as by the slow rate of delivery. They had expected to have the entire set secured by now. Heidemann was asked to see if deliveries could be speeded up.

They could – for a price. With the delivery of the eighteenth diary, on August 22, 1981, Heidemann reported that the price of the diaries had been increased again – by 100 per cent. Each volume would now cost $250,000. Given that each volume contained only about a thousand words, this brought the price to an astounding $250 per word.

Curiously, this didn't bother Gruner and Jahr's executives at all. It simply increased their commitment to the project. Their only response was to increase their project cost estimates, and to give Heidemann a $25,000 bonus.

✦

After years of bouncing cheques and fending off bill-collectors, Heidemann was now swimming in cash. His assets abruptly sky-rocketed. Suddenly he owned a clutch of expensive sports cars, a houseful of costly furniture. He leased two new apartments, one on top of the other, and had them connected. He took his children and fourth wife on a luxury ocean cruise. He bought not one but two vacation villas in Spain. He bought clothes and shoes by the closetful. And he gorged himself on what was fast becoming an out-of-control obsession: the researching and acquisition of further Nazi relics.

He spent $1.3 million refurbishing the *Carin II*. He spent $1 million buying hundreds of paintings and drawings by Hitler. He spent $500,000 digging for buried Nazi treasure in the Stolpsee. He spent a fortune trying to track down Martin Bormann, whose corpse supposedly had been identified in South America by dental records in Germany shortly after the war.

People who knew Heidemann, and who weren't a part of the mysterious new publishing cabal at Gruner and Jahr, shook their heads in amazement.

His colleagues at Gruner and Jahr didn't seem to notice.

They had their own worries.

In February 1982 they had received the twenty-fifth, twenty-sixth, and – unexpectedly – the twenty-seventh Hitler diary. Three weeks later they'd received the twenty-eighth and twenty-ninth. Despite this, certain key periods from 1938, 1941, 1944, and 1945 were still missing. And the cost – now about $5 million – was going through the roof.

Worse, rumours about the diaries had begun to crop up around the publishing industry, and even in the press. It was clear that the lid couldn't be kept on much longer. Yet none of the diaries had yet been checked by either forensic or hand-writing experts.

The company finally decided it couldn't wait any longer. At the risk of losing the remaining diaries – however many that might be – they now contacted archivists at the West German Federal Archives and two internationally known handwriting specialists. They provided each expert with a single page cut from the diaries, but didn't tell them about the diaries themselves. They also enclosed, for comparison purposes, several Hitler documents not related to the diaries but guaranteed by Heidemann to be authentic. (These documents had been acquired from Kujau as well.) Finally, the WGFA also provided each expert with a further three documents from its own files, which its staff had previously authenticated as containing Hitler's own handwriting.

Three weeks later, the results of the first diary examination arrived. Ordway Hilton, a member of the American Board of Forensic Document Examiners, gave it an unqualified thumbs up. This material, he asserted, was genuine Hitler.

Two weeks later the report from the WGFA – which had gone to the Forensic Section of the Rhineland–Pfalz Police Department for its assessment – confirmed Hilton's judgement. Its officials declared "with a probability bordering on certainty" that the Hitler diary excerpt was genuine.

Nine days later, Swiss handwriting-expert Max Frei-Sulzer joined the chorus. "The script of Adolf Hitler," he wrote, "is highly individualistic and offers a good basis for the examination of questionable handwriting . . . there can be no doubt that these documents were written by Adolf Hitler."

At the news, champagne corks popped in *Stern* and Gruner and Jahr offices for an entire week. Anxieties about the snowballing costs of the project and the diaries' dubious provenance evaporated. It was now full steam ahead, with lavish plans for both the announcement and the publication of the diaries. By early 1983, Gruner and Jahr sales agents were fanning out across the Western world to sell syndication and serialization rights. Maximum secrecy was demanded, and all publishers expressing an interest in the project had to sign pledges of strict confidentiality. This, of course, only increased the attraction.

Almost as an afterthought, Thomas Walde, head of *Stern's* history department, followed up on Gruner and Jahr's handwriting authentications by sending a sample of the Hitler diaries (plus several other documents Heidemann had bought from Kujau) to the West German Federal Police for chemical analysis. Rather than an exhaustive examination, which seemed unnecessary in view of the overwhelming vote of confidence by the handwriting experts, he merely asked them to test the age of the paper.

The police, overworked and understaffed, agreed to do the job as soon as they could get to it.

The diaries, meanwhile, kept piling up. By October 1982, there were forty-six. By Christmas there were fifty-one. By March 1983, there were fifty-eight. The tab stood at $10 million and rising, with ancillary costs expected to add at least half that much again.

But by now, nobody at Gruner and Jahr was counting. Publishers on both sides of the Atlantic were crowding in like dealers at Sotheby's, and there seemed no limit to the amount of profit this project could generate. After serialization in magazines there would be a hardcover book, trade-paper editions, mass-market editions, condensed editions; there would be films, recordings, tapes, radio documentaries. Driven by a frenzy of perpetual motion, the project was taking on a life and logic all its own.

Heidemann's assets also kept piling up. In July 1982 he somehow managed to negotiate a further $750,000 from Gruner and Jahr, to pay for some of his more extravagant relics purchases – relics he said he'd been forced to buy to keep his "source" happy – and for Christmas of that year he received "additional compensation" of $375,000, for reasons that nobody seemed able to recall later. He bought himself a million-dollar home in Hamburg's ritziest residential area. He expanded his relic collection to include mementoes of other dictators – Mussolini, Idi Amin – and bought so many new pieces, such as Hitler's suicide weapon and a pair of Idi Amin's underpants, that he had to lease a gallery in downtown Hamburg just to house the collection.

By January 1983 the bidding war for serialization rights to the Hitler diaries had reached maximum intensity. Seesawing furiously, Rupert Murdoch and *Newsweek* magazine were slugging it out in the major leagues, with Murdoch bidding $9.37 million for both the American and the British Commonwealth rights and *Newsweek* offering $7.5 million for the American rights alone. *Paris-Match* carted off the French rights for $1 million. Grupo Zeta beat out all other Spanish bidders at $375,000. Geillustreerde Pers cornered the market for Belgium and Holland at $325,000. Norshe Presse won the Norwegian rights for $125,000. The Italian publishers Mondadori risked $125,000 for four instalments.

It was shaping up to be the biggest syndication deal in publishing history.

And then, on Monday, March 28, a small tremor passed through this fast-rising edifice.

An official of the West German Federal Police finally got back to Thomas Walde about that forensics request. He hoped the long delay hadn't inconvenienced anyone. Things were a bit hectic down at the police laboratories these days. Anyway: the age of the paper of some of the non-diary documents appeared to be quite recent, certainly post-war. They contained a whitening agent called "blankophor," which hadn't been used in pre-war paper. Also, some of the documents contained quite modern glue, and had been typed on a modern typewriter.

Walde took a deep breath. And what about the diary samples? Surely they were pre-war.

Well, of those he wasn't yet sure. He'd have to run some more tests – tests that would require dissolving a small part of each page in a test solution. Would they permit him to snip a small piece off each page for that purpose?

Thomas Walde agreed.

The news sent ripples of suppressed panic through the ranks of the Green Vault group. But the word from Kujau – immediately telephoned by Heidemann – calmed everyone down. They didn't know what the hell they were talking about down there at the WGFP, Kujau assured Heidemann. It was pure nonsense. Paper whitener had been in use in Germany since 1915.

Not knowing whom to believe, Walde decided to wait for the WGFP's further tests. He didn't bother to tell *Stern*'s editors anything about this little problem.

Meanwhile, as *Newsweek*'s and Murdoch's agents jockeyed for position, each brought in its own expert to determine the authenticity of the diaries.

From England, Murdoch's *Sunday Times* hired the acclaimed historian and Third Reich expert Hugh Trevor-Roper. Trevor-Roper had warned Murdoch in advance that he had grave doubts about these diaries. There had never been any indications, in any of the wealth of Third Reich material he'd examined in his lifetime, that Hitler had kept a diary. Besides, it was a well-known fact that Hitler had virtually given up writing anything by hand after 1933.

But on April 8, 1983, when he arrived at the Swiss bank in whose vault Gruner and Jahr now kept the diaries, Trevor-Roper was impressed. The handwriting certainly looked convincing. And the sheer bulk of the diaries – there were by now sixty of them – also struck him as a positive sign. "Who, I asked myself," he said later, "would forge sixty volumes when six would have served his purpose?"

Stern's accompanying sales pitch was no less impressive. Trevor-Roper was shown a detailed dossier tracking the changes in Hitler's signature over the years. He was given the entire story of Gundlfinger's plane crash and the clearly marked graves. He was given the reports of the three handwriting experts. He was also told, inexplicably, that the paper of the diaries had been chemically tested and had proven to be of the right vintage.

When Trevor-Roper returned to his hotel room that afternoon, he telephoned Charles Douglas-Home, editor of one of Murdoch's other British newspapers, the *Times*. "I believe the Hitler diaries are genuine" was his verdict.

Newsweek's expert was now also on his way to Switzerland. University of North Carolina historian Gerhard Weinberg, whose family had fled Hitler's Germany in 1938, had helped compile the U.S. Armed Forces' "Guide to Captured German

Documents" in 1952. He too had his doubts about the diaries, for many of the same reasons as Trevor-Roper, but he acknowledged that "too many things turn up which are not supposed to exist." He agreed to have a closer look at the diaries.

For purposes of comparison, Weinberg had brought along a copy of the unpublished diary of Hitler's valet, Heinz Linge, which covered the second half of 1943. He felt that any major discrepancies between these two documents might indicate authenticity problems. But Hitler's diary for that period was so sketchy that this test proved unworkable. Hitler's entries for other periods with which Weinberg was particularly familiar – the Battle of Stalingrad, for example – proved virtually illegible.

But in general, Weinberg found nothing that jarred or struck a wrong note. He felt that Hitler's signature on virtually every page argued for authenticity, since, he reasoned, no one in his right mind would have risked forging hundreds of Hitler's signatures unnecessarily. And he was delighted to discover an entry covering the Munich Conference of 1938, in which Hitler paid a rather unexpected tribute to British prime minister Neville Chamberlain – calling him a "cunning fox" – which happened to coincide with Weinberg's own unorthodox view of the man.

On his flight back to New York, flanked by two of *Newsweek*'s agents, Weinberg gave his assessment. He was frankly astonished by what he'd been shown. He hadn't been able to detect any obvious flaws. All in all, he considered the diaries genuine.

One week later, Walde got his return phone call from the West German Federal Police chemist who'd been assigned to conduct the tests of the two specimen pages from the Hitler diaries. For good measure, the Federal Archives had also asked him to test one of the additional Kujau documents they had received from *Stern*: a telegram from Hitler to Mussolini.

The chemist essentially confirmed the WGFP's initial findings. The telegram was fake. It contained blankophor.

But the diary pages showed no evidence of blankophor.

The chemist warned, however, that this did not completely exonerate the diary pages; they might have been manufactured after the war without blankophor.

Once again the champagne corks popped in both *Stern* and Gruner and Jahr offices. They were definitely on a roll. Six examinations, six vindications. Now there was nothing in the way of a triumphant, obscenely profitable, all-stops-pulled, spectacular announcement, launch, and sale of the Hitler diaries. The announcement date was set for Friday, April 22, 1983. Publication of the first excerpts, to be launched with a huge press conference in *Stern*'s offices in Hamburg, was set for the following Monday.

✦

At 11:15 on the morning of April 22, 1983, *Stern*'s news department began telexing its announcement of the discovery of the Hitler diaries to the world. *Stern*'s claims were bombastic (if somewhat lacking in English diction): "After evaluation of the diaries, the biography of the dictator, and with it the history of the Nazi state, will have to be written in large part anew."

World reaction was not long in coming, and it was no less opinionated. All the publications which had bought serialization rights hailed the announcement with predictable enthusiasm. Almost everyone else cried foul. Historians throughout the

Western world – especially German historians – were virtually unanimous in their expressions of doubts and derision. "It smacks of pure sensationalism," said German historian Werner Maser. "I'm extraordinarily sceptical," echoed Bonn University's Karl-Dietrich Bracher. Britain's David Irving was even less circumspect. "They're forgeries, pure and simple," he insisted. "I'm shocked that *Stern* would have the gall to publish them."

Reaction at *Stern's* huge press conference three days later was just as sceptical, although this didn't keep news teams from all over the world from attending. Over two hundred of them squashed into *Stern's* large canteen to pelt *Stern's* editor, Peter Koch, with questions. Had the diaries been subjected to exhaustive forensic tests? Had the ink been tested? The paper? Why had no German historians been permitted to examine the diaries? Was their provenance really believable? Who was this mysterious East German source?

Koch's evasive answers threatened to bring the conference down around his ears. But there was worse to come.

Hugh Trevor-Roper used the conference to announce that he was having second thoughts about the diaries. Having only recently discovered how narrowly focused *Stern's* authentication efforts had been, he now felt that the most important tests had been avoided, and this struck him as suspicious. He was publicly withdrawing his vote of confidence in the diaries.

The headlines next morning were devastating.

Alarmed at the growing criticism, *Stern* executives finally made an executive decision. Throwing caution to the wind, they handed over three entire volumes of the diaries to the West German Federal Archives and requested the full treatment: a complete and exhaustive set of historical and forensic tests. They were promised swift and confidential results.

What they got, on May 1, 1983, was certainly swift, but not confidential. The two *Stern* lawyers who arrived at the WGFA to pick up the test results were hit with twin bombshells.

One: *The diaries were totally fake.* Their paper contained chemicals that had not been commercially available before 1955. The ribbons attached to the seals on the covers contained viscose and polyester. The four different kinds of ink used in the diaries were all modern and available at any artists' supply shop. By measuring the degree of chloride evaporation from the ink, forensic chemists had also established that the diaries had been written within the past two years.

Furthermore, textual analysis of the diaries showed them to be littered with historical errors. There were references to laws that hadn't yet been passed on the date of the reference; references to events that hadn't yet taken place. In fact, an alert archivist had even discovered the primary source for the diaries' contents: historian Max Domarus's two-volume edition of *Hitler's Speeches and Proclamations.* Known errors in Domarus's work were invariably repeated in *Stern*'s Hitler diaries.

Two: in view of this incontrovertible evidence of fraud on a national scale, with its serious implications for Germany's international image and reputation, the German government now considered this matter a "ministerial issue." As such, it would be holding an official press conference in precisely one hour to announce its findings to the world.

The two lawyers blanched, and ran for the telephones.

◆

When the dust from the abrupt collapse of *Stern*'s house of cards had cleared enough to show the true dimensions of the disaster, the calls for some honest answers rose to a clamour.

During furious interrogation by Gruner and Jahr executives, Heidemann finally cracked and named Konrad Kujau.

When the police went to arrest Kujau, they believed they were arresting the middleman, a dealer who might be coerced into helping them identify the sophisticated forger who had so brilliantly deceived half a dozen of the world's most accomplished forensic and historical experts. Anyone who knew the poorly educated, barely literate Kujau knew that *he* couldn't have been the forger. He was, as Heidemann put it, "far too primitive."

But when the police searched Kujau's home and business premises on May 13, 1983, they found more than six hundred heavily underlined and annotated books and articles about Hitler, including the already-mentioned Max Domarus works. They found a number of empty notebooks identical to the type used for the Hitler diaries. They also found dozens of Hitler paintings and drawings "in progress" – half-finished, still drying, being aged.

For a while, Kujau stuck to his story that he was just a middleman. But when somebody mentioned that Gruner and Jahr had paid 23 million Deutschmarks (about $11.5 million) for the diaries, he slapped his forehead in disbelief.

"Twenty-three million marks!" he exclaimed, the very picture of righteous outrage. "Twenty-three million marks? That bastard only paid me five!"

That broke the case wide open. Reckless with rage, and determined to keep Heidemann from getting away with his "ill-gotten millions," Kujau admitted his guilt and agreed to turn state's evidence. When Heidemann's lawyer questioned his ability to have forged the diaries, Kujau obligingly gave the court an impromptu demonstration. He'd already amused the police with a similar performance: he had submitted his confession in Hitler's handwriting, signed "Adolf Hitler."

He was, in the amused assessment of one German newspaper, "a thoroughly entertaining rascal," and it showed in the way he handled his own downfall. While Heidemann moped and agonized about his fate – the authorities had impounded everything he owned – Kujau gloried in his newfound fame. During his trial, which drew over 100 reporters and 150 photographers, he played to the audience like a born actor, cheerfully scribbling Hitler diary imitations on any scrap of paper people thrust at him. Naturally, he always signed them "Adolf Hitler."

In prison – both Kujau and Heidemann were sentenced to four and a half years – Kujau kept right on giving interviews, made friends, flirted with every female in sight, and kept everyone royally entertained.

Gerd Heidemann, on the other hand, took prison hard. He spent most of his time in his cell, endlessly poring over a large box of index cards, trying to make sense of the sequence of events that had led to his ruin. Whatever else he'd done, he had always devoutly believed the Hitler diaries to be genuine. The revelation of their inauthenticity now shook him like a religious crisis. Sometimes, unable to ignore the sounds of Kujau regaling yet another group of reporters or inmates with his hilarious tales of mischievous crookery – both men had cells on the same prison range – he would clutch his head and let out a howl of outrage, ending in an agonized moan. He eventually suffered a nervous breakdown and spent time in the prison's psychiatric unit.

Over at *Stern*, and at Gruner and Jahr, the shouts, pounding fists, and flying memos conveyed the sounds of denial, self-justification, and much finger-pointing. By the time the tumult had settled, several heads had rolled – not the most blameworthy ones, apparently – and the company had to fork out another $7 million to avoid two wrongful dismissal suits. They also had to return all the money they'd received for the diaries' serialization rights.

All told, the whole débâcle appears to have cost these publishing houses about $24 million.

Only Konrad Kujau, alias Konrad Fischer, alias Peter Fischer, alias Heinz Fischer, a.k.a. "The General," sarcastically called "The Professor," known to his friends simply as "Conny," the least-educated, least-sophisticated, lowest-class actor in this post-Hitlerian drama, climbed out of the wreckage of the Hitler diaries fiasco apparently unscathed.

Most of the $3 million he'd received for his forgeries was never recovered. He served his time in prison as if it were one long, uninterrupted party. And when he got out, he sold his life story to Germany's *Bild Zeitung* newspaper for $125,000.

Sources

1. RUNNING AWAY WITH MONA

Karl Decker, "Why and How the Mona Lisa Was Stolen,"
Saturday Evening Post, June 25, 1932.

Milton Esterow, *The Art Stealers*, Macmillan, New York, 1973

Roy McMullan, *Mona Lisa: The Picture and the Myth*, Houghton
Mifflin, Boston, 1975.

Seymour Reit, *The Day They Stole the Mona Lisa*, Summit
Books, New York, 1981.

2. ROBBING ARIZONA TO PAY JAMES

Alexander Klein, ed. *Grand Deception*, Lippincott, Philadelphia,
1955.

Egon Larsen, *The Deceivers*, Roy Publishers, New York, 1966.

Donald M. Powell, *The Peralta Land Grant*, University of
Oklahoma Press, Norman, 1960.

Scoundrels & Scalawags, Reader's Digest Assn., New York, 1968.

3. POT O' MAGIC TRADEMARKS

David Mulligan, *Eire As She Lives and Breathes*, Ramsey Publications, London, 1987.

Colin Rose, ed., *The World's Greatest Rip-Offs*, Sterling Publishing, New York, 1978.

4. SALAD-OIL KING OF THE UNIVERSE

N. C. Miller, *The Great Salad Oil Swindle*, Coward McCann, New York, 1965.

Carl Sikakis, *Hoaxes and Scams*, Facts on File, New York, 1993.

5. THE FLEA THAT ROARED

Harry Bruce, "Old Baldy," *Weekend* magazine, March 29, 1975.

Alexander Klein, ed., *Grand Deception*, Lippincott, Philadelphia, 1955.

6. PIG IN A POKE

Colin Rose, ed., *The World's Greatest Rip-Offs*, Sterling Publishing, New York, 1978.

7. BOGUS BIRDMAN OF BRONXVILLE

Frank Abagnale and Stan Redding, *Catch Me If You Can*, Grosset & Dunlap, New York, 1980.

8. OIL'S WELL THAT ENDS WELL

David McClintick, *Stealing from the Rich*, M. Evans & Company, New York, 1977.

9. THE PHARAOH OF PYRAMID SELLING

John Frasca, *Glenn Turner: Con Man or Saint?* Self-published, n.d.

The Great American Mail-Fraud Trial: U.S.A. Versus Glenn W. Turner. Nash Publications, New York, 1976.

Rudy Maxa, *Dare to Be Great*, William Morrow, New York, 1977.

also: *The Marion Star*, 1970–1972, Marion, South Carolina.

10. FROZEN ASSETS

Nigel Blundell, *The World's Greatest Crooks & Conmen*, Octopus, London, 1982.

Harold Simons, ed., *Those College Highjinks*, Marshall Press, Chicago, 1980.

11. THE GREAT PUROLATOR PAPER CAPER

Tony Marzano and Painter Powell, *The Big Steal*, Houghton Mifflin, Boston, 1980.

also: *Chicago Tribune*, October 21 to November 29, 1974, and April 15 to 18, 1975.

12. FOR EXPORT ONLY

Colin Rose, ed., *The World's Greatest Rip-Offs*, Sterling Publishing, New York, 1978.

also: *The Times*, London, March 14, 1961.

13. BRAND-NAME CRIME

Albert Spaggiari, *Fric-Frac: The Great Riviera Bank Robbery*, Martin Sokolinsky, trans., Houghton Mifflin, Boston, 1979.

14. DRUNK AND DISORDERLY

Nigel Blundell, *The World's Greatest Crooks & Conmen*, Octopus, London, 1982.

Curtis McDougall, *Hoaxes*, Dover Publishing, New York, 1958.

15. THE MAN WHO FELL FROM THE SKY

Max Gunther, *D. B. Cooper: What Really Happened*, Contemporary Books, Chicago, 1985.

Ralph Himmelsbach, *Norjak: The Investigation of D. B. Cooper*, Norjak Project, Salt Lake City, 1986.

Bernie Rhodes, *D. B. Cooper: The Real McCoy*, University of Utah Press, Salt Lake City, 1991.

16. VIRTUAL WHIPLASH

Peter Kerr, "Ghost Riders Haunt Insurers, Bus Operators," N.Y. Times News Service, *The Oregonian*, Friday, August 20, 1993.

17. HITLER FOR SALE

Robert Harris, *Selling Hitler: Story of the Hitler Diaries*, Faber and Faber, London, 1986.

Author photo: Sharon Brown

Born in 1946, Andreas Schroeder grew up in British Columbia and attended U.B.C. A well-known figure in the literary community, he has served as literary critic of the Vancouver *Province*, co-founder/director of the *Canadian Fiction Magazine*, and co-founder/editor of *Contemporary Literature in Translation*. He has taught Creative Writing at Simon Fraser University, the University of Victoria, and the University of Winnipeg. He currently shares the Maclean-Hunter Chair in Creative Non-fiction at the University of British Columbia.

He has published over a dozen books, including *File of Uncertainties* (poetry), *The Late Man* (short fiction), *Dust Ship Glory* (novel), and *The Eleventh Commandment* (translation). His memoir, *Shaking It Rough*, was nominated for the Governor General's Award in 1976. His fiction and poetry have been included in over forty anthologies, and his byline has appeared in most Canadian magazines and newspapers. In 1991 he was awarded the Canadian Association of Journalists' Best Investigative Journalism Award.

In addition to his writing, he has been a regular broadcaster for CBC Radio – most notably on "Basic Black" – and a tireless crusader for writers' benefits in Canada. He served as Chairman of the Writers' Union of Canada in 1975-76, and as the founding Chair of Canada's Public Lending Right Commission in 1986-88.

Andreas Schroeder lives in Mission, B.C., with his wife, Sharon Brown, and their two daughters, Sabrina and Vanessa.